CHRISTIAN CHARACTER:

REMADE IN THE IMAGE OF GOD

· VOLUME ONE ·

FRANK MARTIN

Christian Character: Remade in the Image of God
Copyright © 2016 by Frank Martin
Revised edition

Edited by Adam Colwell
Interior design and typesetting by Katherine Lloyd
Cover Design by Caryn Metcalf
Published by Adam Colwell's WriteWorks LLC

Printed in the United States of America
www.martins4turkey.com

∾

This book is dedicated to my children,
Amy and Matthew, whom I love dearly.

Special thanks to my wife, Caroline,
for her patience in seeing this volume completed.

Special thanks also to David Phillips, who did
the first editing on the manuscript, and to Adam Colwell,
who was the final editor. They both sacrificed much time
and effort to helping this book come to completion.

CONTENTS

JOIN THE QUEST

S ocieties are changed only when people are changed, not the other way around. The crisis is not political; it is moral and spiritual. And so is the solution."[1]

That truth, stated by Charles Colson, forms the basis for *Christian Character, Remade in the Image of God.* We will change only through the work of God's Holy Spirit in our lives, and as we are changed, we will look, think, feel, and act like Jesus.

I first discovered the vital need for character in the lives of Christians back in 1971 when I was a young believer attending a Sunday potluck lunch that was likely far different than any you've ever attended—because it took place while living on a hippie commune.

The green, hilly farm in southern Oregon that hosted the commune was bordered by tall pines and punctuated by a main house. By the river that ran alongside the vast swath of land was a series of dwellings: cabins, trailers, shacks, and the occasional tent. Living in these diverse homesteads were couples who worked together, ate together, and played together.

A commune was the last place I thought I'd ever live when I was growing up in small town Ohio, dutifully attending an Episcopal church, and learning from the rector there that, while Jesus was a great teacher and role model, the Bible was more allegory than fact. I found church to

---

1 Colson, p. 11.

be stuffy, dull, and definitely not cool. I stopped going as a teenager and had no plans to return.

I ended up in college studying business at Miami University in Oxford, Ohio. In my sophomore year I met Caroline, and she was the second person in my life, after my mother, that I could really talk to. We wed three days after we graduated. We settled in Tucson, Arizona, where Caroline became a teacher in nearby Tubac. I started grad school at the University of Arizona and met a Peace Corps recruiter on campus. Not long afterward, Caroline and I decided to join the Peace Corps and, only one year after moving to the southwestern desert, we found ourselves on a plane to the Middle East, specifically Turkey.

The contrast between the Muslim culture and the one I knew in the United States created a discord in my soul. I felt a sense of oppression that was displayed in the way the people both looked and acted as they lived out their lives in a religious system that denied personal freedom and had little to no regard for the value of human life. I wanted to help the Turkish people, but realized I didn't have anything to offer that could make a difference in their lives. Through my Peace Corps work, I was providing them with an understanding of the tourism industry and how to profit from foreign visitors—but to what end? I might help their standard of living, but their bondage would continue. I felt inadequate, powerless, and lacking answers to the questions their plight presented: *Who am I? Why am I here? What is the meaning of life?*

Caroline and I returned to the United States and we started a quest to answer those questions. Based on my childhood church experiences, I didn't think Christianity was a solution, so we looked elsewhere: transcendental meditation, eastern religions, modern psychology. We intuitively knew "truth" existed, but it was elusive. That search led us to the hills of the hippie commune—and to a couple who invited us to a Bible study taught by an ex-drug dealer from California.

Inside a log cabin beside the river, Caroline and I asked all kinds of question about the Bible and Jesus. When we returned to our single-wide trailer home, we contemplated what we learned and tried to come up with reasons why we shouldn't accept Jesus Christ as Savior.

We couldn't. Two weeks later we were born again—and redirected our quest to seek truth from the One who calls Himself "The Truth." We began to attend a small country church in a nearby town that welcomed all of us hippies with open arms. It was glorious!

Then came the Sunday potluck lunch—and the argument we witnessed between two older people in the church. They angrily debated which one of them was the most spiritually mature. At one point, they were so upset they screamed at each other. It was a wake-up call. I thought that when a person became a Christian, their character was instantly remade to reflect Christ's character. That incident convinced me I was wrong. Christian character doesn't just happen automatically. It's something that God develops within us through the work of the Holy Spirit.

> I thought that when a person became a Christian, their character was instantly remade to reflect His character. I was wrong.

∾

The essential component of Christian maturity is love for God and love for each other. Yet the quest of spiritual growth is not an easy process. It's one we have to work at our entire lives. As I've gone through this process in the forty-six years since that day at the potluck, I've also realized that a profound lack of character exists in our culture, in our schools, and in our homes. The United States and other great nations have lost their spiritual foundation in God and have since reaped the consequences of trading faith in God for faith in self.

What went wrong? President Abraham Lincoln, in his Proclamation of Humiliation, Fasting and Prayer speech on April 30, 1863, said, "We have been preserved these many years in peace and prosperity. We have grown in numbers, wealth, and power as no other nation has ever grown. But we have forgotten God. We have forgotten the gracious hand which preserved us in peace and multiplied and enriched and strengthened us; and we have vainly imagined, in the deceitfulness of our hearts, that all these blessings were produced by some superior wisdom and virtue of our own. Intoxicated with unbroken success, we have become too self-sufficient to feel the necessity of redeeming and preserving grace, too proud to pray to the God that made us."[2]

Alexander Solzhenitsyn, the Russian historian and writer, said in a speech as he received the Templeton Prize in Religion in 1981:

"Over a half a century ago, while I was still a child, I recall hearing a number of older people offer the following explanation for the great disaster that had befallen Russia: 'Men have forgotten God; that's why all this has happened.' Since then I have spent well-nigh fifty years working on the history of our revolution; in the process I have read hundreds of books, collected hundreds of personal testimonies, and have already contributed eight volumes of my own toward the effort of clearing away the rubble left by the upheaval. But if I were asked today to formulate as concisely as possible the main cause of the ruinous revolution that swallowed up some sixty million of our people, I could not put it more accurately than to repeat: 'Men have forgotten God; that's why all this happened.'"[3]

> We have forgotten God and are reaping the fruit of our actions.

In his 1999 book "Against the Night," Charles Colson states that "a crisis of immense proportion is upon us. Not from the threat of nuclear holocaust or a stock market collapse, not from the greenhouse effect or trade deficits, not from East-West relations or ferment in the Middle East." He continues: "The crisis that threatens us, the force that could topple our monuments and destroy our very foundations, is within ourselves. The crisis is in the character of our culture, where the values that restrain inner vices and develop inner virtues are eroding."[4] He then writes of the "new barbarians" in Western culture, invaders from within. "We have bred them in our families and trained them in our classrooms. They inhabit our legislatures, our courts, our film studios, and our churches."[5]

2 Thomas, p.. 27.
3 Thomas, p. 27, 28.
4 Colson, pp. 10, 11.
5 Ibid, pp. 23, 24.

JOIN THE QUEST | 11

Our culture has moved increasingly toward secularism and hedonism—and it is revealed in the character of the people. Sadly, we have forgotten God and are reaping the fruit of our actions. Romans 1:18-23 points out that God has made His presence clear for everyone to see, but men "neither glorified him as God nor gave thanks to him." When we turn from God, we turn *toward* depravity in our thinking, darkness in our understanding, humanism in our worldview, deadness in our worship, and broken relationships in our homes.[6] We don't even recognize Godly character, let alone possess it. The moral heritage of our civilization has shifted to where we are looking at how to fix symptoms rather than addressing the underlying, philosophical problems. We have abandoned God—abandoned truth—and therefore have no moral compass. Christian character is the casualty.

If the fruit of turning away from God is a general ungodliness in our character, imagine what it looks like when God restores His people to the likeness of Christ. The end result of spiritual growth is spiritual maturity. Yet what is Christian character? What does a mature Christian look like? What are the core qualities of a mature believer, according to Scripture?

Christian Character: Remade in the Image of God is not a book about the process alone; rather, it's about what we look like when the process is completed (even though the process is not fully finished until we go to Heaven to be with the Lord). It is a guide book for those of us who want to understand what it looks like to be restored to the image of God. My hope is that it will stimulate you to keep on the path of inner transformation and will help you to be part of the answer to the moral decline in our culture.

Join me on this quest as we, in cooperation with God's Holy Spirit, develop Christian character, strive for maturity that shows itself in our love for God and love for each other—and truly make a difference in people's lives.

---

6 Romans 1:29-31 *They have become filled with every kind of wickedness, evil, greed and depravity. They are full of envy, murder, strife, deceit and malice. They are gossips, slanderers, God-haters, insolent, arrogant and boastful; they invent ways of doing evil; they disobey their parents; they are senseless, faithless, heartless, ruthless.*

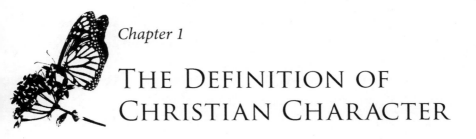

Chapter 1

THE DEFINITION OF CHRISTIAN CHARACTER

O ur model of character, whether we acknowledge God or not, comes from God. Jesus said that if we knew Him—that is, if we knew what Christ is really like—we would know what God is really like (John 8:19; John 14:7). Christ was God manifested in the flesh. He is the embodiment of Godly character. Yet if someone were to ask you to describe what Christian character is, you would probably list the characteristics of a spiritually mature person you know. Why? We know character from people.

When I began attending a large church in Tucson, Arizona that offered Bible college courses, I took every class I could: church history, hermeneutics, introductions to the Old and New Testaments, systematic theology, etc. I was eager to learn and soak up all the information. However, the real transformation in my life came not from the content, but the teachers. I became good friends with one of the instructors and I observed his love for the Lord as well as his relationship with his children, his wife, and the church. He didn't just talk about Christ; he had a deep and long-term relationship with Him and lived out the Christian life every day. I was a new Christian and I knew that my new life in Jesus was to be totally different—but it was by watching a more mature believer that I learned what that difference really looked like in day-to-day life. He is still a friend, and I have seen him walk faithfully with the Lord through many difficult seasons of life.

I have heard people say that we get character by osmosis. We are not changed by theory and principles alone, but by encountering people who are spiritually mature and, therefore, exhibit Christian character.

Character defined

Webster's Dictionary defines character as a distinctive mark, trait, quality, or attribute; an essential quality; an individual's pattern of behavior or personality; and as moral strength, self-discipline, and fortitude.[1] Bible teacher and author Charles Swindoll defines character as "the moral, ethical, and spiritual undergirding that rests on truth that reinforces a life in stressful times, and resists all temptations to compromise."[2]

> Character is manifested both in the vertical (toward God) and horizontal (toward men) directions.

Evangelist and publisher Dwight L. Moody said character is "what you are in the dark."

Author and social critic Oz Guinness says that there are three distinguishing characteristics of character:

1. Core: Character is the essential "stuff" a person is made of, the inner reality in which thoughts, speech, decisions, behavior, and relations are rooted. "Just as a nation's constitution expresses its fundamental character and makeup, so a person's character expresses most deeply what constitutes him or her as a unique individual."

2. Consistency: One's character is best seen in what a person reveals consistently rather than in a single statement or random act. French political thinker and historian Alexis-Charles-Henri Clérel de Tocqueville calls it the "habits of the heart." German philosopher Friedrich Nietzsche calls it a long obedience in the same direction.

3. Cost: Consistent core-character is normally formed best and revealed most clearly in the crucible of testing.[3]

---

1   Webster's Dictionary, article on "character", 1983 edition.
2   Swindohl, p. 66.
3   Guinness, *When No One Sees*, p. 16.

Perhaps the concept of Christian character is best illustrated by Oswald, king of Northumbria in the seventh century, who said this of Aidan, a monk: "He helped me to see how to be a practical Christian and turn my faith into action. I'll never forget the look on the hungry warriors' faces when I gave our Easter dinner away to the poor! But Aidan was thrilled. He's genuine through and through, is Aidan. There's no difference between what he teaches and what he is."[4]

Character Profile
Joseph - Integrity

When Joseph, the son of Jacob, was 17 years old, Jacob made him a coat of many colors. Jacob loved Joseph more than the other 11 brothers so the brothers became jealous of Joseph. They sold him into slavery to the Midianites, who sold him to Potiphar, the captain of Pharaoh's guard. The Lord was with Joseph and everything he did was done with integrity and success. Potiphar made Joseph overseer of everything he had and Potiphar prospered in everything with Joseph in charge. Joseph was well built and handsome, so Potiphar's wife wanted him to have sex with her. He refused. One day, when Joseph and Potiphar's wife were alone in the house, she caught him by his garment and asked him to lie with her (Genesis 39:12). He fled, leaving his garment in her hand. She lied to her husband that Joseph had tried to rape her, leaving his garment behind. Potiphar believed his wife and had Joseph thrown into prison.

We see in this story Joseph's integrity. He was a young man with all the sexual desires of men his age, but he refused to compromise his integrity by going to bed with someone else's wife. He was committed to sexual purity and to doing what is right in the eyes of the Lord. It is very important that we also, as believers,

---

4   Celtic Daily Prayer, *Prayers and Readings from the North Umbria Community*, HarperCollins Publishers, September 3 reading, p. 495.

are committed to sexual purity. Many Christian leaders have been brought down through giving in to sexual temptation and committing adultery. Their ministries have been ruined. 1 Corinthians 6:18 says: "Flee from sexual immorality. All other sins a person commits are outside the body, but whoever sins sexually, sins against their own body." Colossians 3:5 says "Put to death, therefore, whatever belongs to your earthly nature: sexual immorality, impurity, lust, evil desires and greed, which is idolatry." We need to commit ourselves to sexual purity throughout our lives. We are to do what it takes, as Joseph did, to avoid getting tangled up in the web of sexual sin.

Character is manifested both in the vertical (toward God) and horizontal (toward men) directions; we are to have integrity before God, but also integrity before other people. "Live such good lives among the pagans that, though they accuse you of doing wrong, they may see your good deeds and glorify God on the day he visits us." (1 Peter 2:12; Read also Matthew 22:36-39; 1 Peter 3:1-2)

James Davison Hunter, sociologist and professor of religion, culture, and social theory at the University of Virginia, says this character consists of three elements:

1. Moral discipline: the inner capacity for restraint; an ability to inhibit oneself in one's passions, desires, and habits within the boundaries of a moral order.
2. Moral attachment: the affirmation of our commitments to a large community, the embrace of an ideal that attracts us, draws us, animates us, and inspires us.
3. Moral autonomy: a person's capacity to freely make ethical decisions.[5]

---

5   Hunter, p. 16.

Hunter goes on to say that character "manifests itself as the autonomy to make ethical decisions always on behalf of the common good and the discipline to abide by that principle."[6]

Character, then, is what we are when no one sees but God. It is our essential quality, our moral constitution, and our ethical and spiritual undergirding that rests on truth and reinforces a life in stressful times and resists all temptations to compromise. Even more, Christian character is the *endpoint* that results in being a spiritually mature believer. It is the place of peace with God, with ourselves, and with other men.

The difference between character and personality

Godly character is what God is making each of us into; it's the same for every person on the face of the Earth. Everyone is to exhibit the fruit of the Holy Spirit and be loving, patient, kind, joyful, as so on (Read Galatians 5:22-23). There is only one image of Christ and all of us everywhere are being transformed into that image. A Chinese villager is being transformed into a person with love, joy, and peace in the same way as a stockbroker in New York City.

Personality, however, is the unique blend of traits which God has given to each of us. Merriam-Webster defines personality as "the totality of an individual's behavioral and emotional characteristics; a set of distinctive traits.[7] Some people have a great sense of humor, others are very serious; some are outgoing, others are introverted; some are take-charge kinds of people, others are followers. God is not trying to change our personality, but rather bring out the *best* of our personality through the work of His Spirit. Our personality is unique, distinct, and a gift from God. He only wants to make you a transformed you. He designed you the way He wants you to be, and as you mature in Christ your basic personality will be refined, but not changed. Just as your hair color, eye color, and ethnicity doesn't change as you mature in Christ, your personality continues to be the same—but your uniqueness comes out like a flower when you accept

6   Ibid, p. 17.
7   Merriam-Webster online dictionary: http://www.merriam-webster.com/dictionary/personality.

the work of God in you to remake you into the image of Christ and exhibit is character.

How roles develop character

Each of us has roles to play: parent, spouse, neighbor, student, worker. Each of those roles has behaviors and attitudes conducive to the role. A father is to take care of his family and provide for them. A mother is to nurture her children. A worker is to work diligently. But there is a character *ideal* expressed in each of those roles, sometimes in different ways. We are to be honest, humble, loving, and joyful.

Christian character is not easy to attain.

However, our honesty as a neighbor might be expressed in returning a borrowed tool, whereas as a father I keep my word to my children. My humility as a husband might look different than it would as a student. The role defines how the character quality is expressed.

Roles are also where different character qualities are developed. I learned how to be more patient through being a father. I discovered the meaning of true sacrificial love through raising two children; in fact, I never understood the Father's love until I had my own children. I learned diligence through being a student. I learned how to listen to others through my marriage. There are also unique character qualities to each of the roles the Lord has given us. Husbands are to love their wives and nurture their children. Wives are to respect their husbands. Children are to obey their parents. Citizens are to pray for their leaders. Our roles are the training ground to develop certain qualities in our character. All of us are in God's school to teach us different aspects of His multi-dimensional character.

The difficulty of Christian character and spiritual maturity

Christian character is not easy to attain. It involves death to self, separating from the world, and giving up everything to walk with Christ. It is a life of death and joy, pain and glory. But there is within us a part that wants to call the shots, exalt ourselves, and live a comfortable life.

Jesus didn't come to make us miserable, but He did call us to put to death the sins of the flesh (Read Romans 8:1-11). He knows that it is our sinful nature that keeps us from living a life pleasing to God. We have to give up ownership of our happiness and the claim to our own rights, and turn them over to an unseen God whom we believe by faith will give us a better, more fulfilling life (Read John 10:10; Romans 8:12-14) But we have to give up before we regain. We have to die before we live. Evangelist and teacher Oswald Chambers, author of "My Utmost for His Highest," said "the inescapable spiritual need each of us has is the need to sign the death certificate of our sin nature. I must take my emotional opinions and intellectual beliefs and be willing to turn them into a moral verdict against the nature of sin; that is, against any claim I have to my right to myself."[8]

Our salvation is a free gift of God. (Read Ephesians 2:8-9) There is nothing we can do to merit salvation. It is something which God did to demonstrate the depth of His love and grace. Man and woman, boy and girl, rich and poor, powerful and powerless all stand equal as a result of God's justifying grace.

However, all do not have the same character flaws to overcome. The murderer who is justified by Christ has the same standing before God as the pastor who grew up in a Christian home, but the murderer might have some serious character issues. The murderer might have grown up in an abusive, unloving, and ungodly home. He might have anger to overcome or be resentful of authority. In the Bible, Paul was a murderer, yet he was justified by the Lord and became one of the great early leaders of the Christian church. The penalty for sin has been dealt with on the cross once and for all, but the pollution of sin is not equal. Each of us needs salvation through Christ, but we have different things to overcome in our character.

None of these character issues are impossible for the Holy Spirit to deal with, but it will not come easily. All of us have to die to self. The murderer can become a great Christian leader. That is the grace of God.

---

8 Chambers, *My Utmost*, March 17.

But it will take a deep work of the Holy Spirit to transform us from the inside out. We cannot get by with what German Lutheran pastor, theologian, and anti-Nazi dissident Dietrich Bonhoeffer calls cheap grace, "the preaching of forgiveness without requiring repentance, baptism without church discipline, Communion without confession, absolution without personal confession. Cheap grace is grace without discipleship … Costly grace is the treasure hidden in the field; for the sake of it a man will gladly go and sell all that he has. It is the pearl of great price to buy for which the merchant will sell all his goods. It is the kingly rule of Christ."[9]

"I have been crucified with Christ and I no longer live, but Christ lives in me. The life I live in the body, I live by faith in the Son of God, who loved me and gave himself for me." (Galatians 2:20; Read also Matthew 10:34-39; Luke 14:26-27; John 12:24-25) To be a disciple of Jesus and to pursue spiritual maturity requires you to travel a narrow way (Read Matthew 7:13-14). It's a lifelong pursuit which involves suffering, disappointment, and loss—but also great joy. The losses are temporal, but the gains are eternal.

Bonhoeffer elaborates: "A little band of men, the followers of Christ, are separated from the rest of the world. The disciples are few in number, and will always be few … To believe the promise of Jesus that his followers shall possess the earth, and at the same time to face our enemies unarmed and defenseless, preferring to incur injustice rather than to do wrong ourselves, is indeed a narrow way. To see the weakness and wrong in others, and at the same time refrain from judging them; to deliver the gospel message without casting pearls before swine, is indeed a narrow way.[10]

Quaker theologian and author Richard Foster says "the desperate need today is not for a greater number of intelligent people, or gifted people, but for deep people. Deep people have allowed God to work in their lives and are not afraid to be changed into the image of Christ.

---

9 Bonhoeffer, *Cost of Discipleship*, p. 47.
10 Ibid, p. 211.

Those who possess depth of character have gone through life walking with God and have been transformed into the image of Christ, who was and is very deep."[11]

Character Profile
Ruth - Loyalty

The story of Ruth takes place in the time of the Judges, after the Israelites had been in the Promised Land for some time. A man named Elimelek, from the town of Bethlehem, and his wife Naomi had two sons. When there was a famine in the land of Israel, Elimelek took his family to the land of Moab. While there for about 10 years, their two sons married Moabite women, one of whom was Ruth. Elimelek and the two sons died, leaving Naomi with her two daughters-in-law. When there was food again in Israel, Naomi left to go back home. Naomi urged her daughters-in-law to go back to Moab, but Ruth refused to leave Naomi's side and replied, "Don't urge me to leave you or to turn back from you. Where you go I will go, and where you stay I will stay. Your people will be my people and your God my God. Where you die I will die, and there I will be buried. May the LORD deal with me, be it ever so severely, if even death separates you and me." (Ruth 1:16,17) Ruth went on to marry Boaz and they became the progenitors of king David, and therefore of Christ.

How does this relate to us? Love is loyal. 1 Corinthians 13:7 says, "Love never gives up, never loses faith, is always hopeful, and endures through every circumstance. "(NLT) We as believers are called to loyalty, both to God and to other people. I am convinced that one reason for the breakup of marriages in our day is a lack of loyalty to God and to our spouses. We are called to bloom where we are planted. Let us practice loyalty to one another.

---

11 Foster, *Celebration of Discipline*, p. 1.

Old and New Testament words which talk about character

In this section we will look at both the Old and the New Testament words and concepts which refer to character.

OT words used to refer to character

1. *hayil*

The first Hebrew word used to refer to "character"[12] is found in Ruth 3:11, Proverbs 12:4 and Proverbs 31:10. The word means literally "a woman of might, strength, ability, efficiency, wealth." It's also used to refer to moral worth or virtue. The basic meaning of the word is strength.[13] Thus, Ruth was a strong woman, and Proverbs talks about how a wife of noble character is worth more than rubies.

2. *tamim*

The second word in the Hebrew is *tamim*.[14] The fundamental meaning of *tamim* is completeness or wholeness. Noah was *tamim*, or blameless (Genesis 6:9). God exhorted Abraham to be blameless (Genesis 17:1). Animal sacrifices were to be without defect (same Hebrew word used). Christ was perfect, blameless, without defect (without sin) and so He could be the perfect sacrifice for sin.

3. *shalem*

The third word used in the Hebrew text was *shalem*,[15] a word used over 250 times in the Old Testament. It is translated *peace*, or *well-being* in the NIV text. The general meaning behind the root is that of completion and fulfillment—of entering into a state of wholeness and unity, a restored relationship.[16] The noun form of *shalem* is *shalom*, which means "completeness, wholeness, harmony, fulfillment."[17] The meaning is that of unimpaired relationships with others and fulfillment in

---

12 חַיִל (*hayil*) in the Hebrew.
13 TWOT, article on חַיִל (*hayil*) by Carl Philip Weber.
14 תָּמִים in the Hebrew.
15 שָׁלֵם in the Hebrew.
16 TWOT, Vol 2, pp 930-932.
17 Ibid, 931.

one's undertakings. It means absence of strife. The word is also used as a greeting for "hello" and "goodbye" in modern Hebrew. To wish someone *shalom* was to wish them a blessing.

In nearly two-thirds of its occurrences, *shalom* describes the state of fulfillment which is the result of God's presence.[18] The only sort of *shalom* which is possible is that which God initiates and which results in communion or peace with Him. Christ is the Messiah, the Prince of Peace, the one who brings fulfillment and righteousness to the earth.[19] Christ, then becomes our righteousness, destroying the hostility between sinful man and God.

The word is also used to refer to the peace offering or thank offering in the Old Testament sacrificial system. When the priest offered an offering of peace, God conferred on the one who offered the offering the gift of wholeness, prosperity, and the status of being at peace with God. This involves more than forgiveness of sin, in that fullness of life, prosperity, and peace with men is the expected result of *shalom* status. [20]Christ became sin for us so that we could enjoy peace, wholeness, justification before God, and prosperity in our souls.

Some conclusions about the Old Testament words

a. These three Old Testament words each have a little different slant on what character is about as revealed in the OT. *hayil* is about strength or valor, *tamim* is about completeness or wholeness, *shalem* is a state of wholeness or fulfillment, unimpaired relationships with others. Character encompasses all of these concepts. The person who has Godly character is strong and virtuous, complete, whole, and he/she has unimpaired relationships with others, including God.

b. The entire OT is a commentary on the character of God. A theme that runs through the whole OT is the development of what God is like. Different aspects of His character are revealed in the lives of Noah, the

---

18 Ibid, 931.
19 Ibid, 931.
20 Ibid, 932.

patriarchs (Abraham, Isaac, Jacob, Joseph), Moses, Ruth, Naomi and Boaz, David, Abigail, Solomon, Nehemiah, Ezra, Esther, Job and the prophets. Then there are all the negative examples of character, men and women like Cain, Esau, the Pharoah of Egypt, King Saul, Haman, Nabal, the kings of the Northern Kingdom of Israel and many of the kings of the Southern Kingdom. Special attention is given to some who were especially evil, like Nabal, Ahab, and Jezebel. There is also a whole lot revealed about God's character in the Psalms, Proverbs, Ecclesiastes and the Song of Songs. God was calling the men and women of the Old Testament to become like Him.

c. The stories of the OT were written so that we could learn what constitutes Godly character. Some of the stories were given to inspire us to become better people (like the story of Joseph) and some to warn us about straying from the path of understanding (like Ahab). In the story about Joseph, for example, we see Joseph's patience in waiting on God to deliver him from very difficult circumstances (being sold into slavery, spending many years in prison); we see Joseph's extraordinary forgiveness of his brothers for first wanting to kill him, then selling him into slavery; we see Joseph's recognition of God's sovereignty; we see his integrity, not giving into temptation and commitment to moral purity when enticed by Potiphar's wife; we see his diligence to administrative detail when he was in charge of Potiphar's household, when he was put in charge of the rest of the prisoners in the jail, and when he became second in command over all Egypt.

d. We recognize Godly character when we see it in scripture, but we also see it in the lives of the people around us. None of us are or will be like Christ, but we can see aspects of Christ's character in each other.

NT words referring to character

In the New Testament, we discover that Christian character is just the extension of this Old Testament concept of completion, perfection, and peace. There are 4 Greek words in the NIV which refer to character, and then there are other synonyms which refer to character.

1. "Now the Bereans were of more noble character than the Thessalonians, for they received the message with great eagerness and examined the Scriptures every day to see if what Paul said was true." (Acts 17:11) The word translated "character" in Acts 17:11 is *eugenys*[21] which means "having a high status, socially well-born, noble; a nobleman, an important person." It can also signify "a commendable attitude, open-minded, without prejudice, or more open-minded, less prejudiced."

2. "Not only so, but we also rejoice in our sufferings, because we know that suffering produces perseverance; perseverance, character; and character, hope." (Romans 5:3,4) The word translated "character" (in the NIV) in Romans 5:4 is *dokimyn*,[22] which means "having the quality of having stood the test, mature or approved character."

3. "Do not be misled: "Bad company corrupts good character." (1 Corinthians 15:33) The Greek word for character in 1 Corinthians 15:33 is *ethos*,[23] which means a fixed pattern of behavior "habit, custom, usage." In the plural it means "morals, habits, character." The English word comes from the root *sweth* and the Latin word *seutus*, which means "accustomed, customary." The key concept is "customary," that which we do out of habit.

The word *ethos* is used twelve times in the New Testament and is the word from which we derive the English word "ethos," which Webster's Dictionary defines as "the fundamental character of spirit of a culture; the underlying sentiment that informs the beliefs, customs, or practices of a group or society; the distinguishing character or disposition of a community, group, person; the moral element in dramatic literature that determines a character's action or behavior."

4. "Perseverance must finish its work so that you may be mature and complete, not lacking anything." (James 1:4) The word used in James 1:4 in the New Testament is the Greek root *tel*. Seven times it is translated

---

21 εὐγενής in the Greek.
22 δοκιμήν in the Greek.
23 ἦθος in the Greek.

"mature" in the New International Version and ten times it is translated "perfect." Luke 8:14 says, "The seed that fell among thorns stands for those who hear, but as they go on their way they are choked by life's worries, riches and pleasures, and <u>they do not mature</u>." It means "bring to maturity;" of fruit "bring to ripeness, produce ripe fruit;" used metaphorically of spiritual character in this passage, meaning "become all that one should be." In this passage, then, the sense is that the mature are those who have come to ripeness, who have become all that God has intended for them. Other passages include:

- "Epaphras, who is one of you and a servant of Christ Jesus, sends greetings. He is always wrestling in prayer for you, that you may stand firm in all the will of God, mature and fully assured." (Colossians 4:12)
- "But solid food is for the mature, who by constant use have trained themselves to distinguish good from evil." (Hebrews 5:14)
- Read also 1 Corinthians 2:6; Ephesians 4:13; Philippians 3:15

All these passages use the Greek word *teleios*,[24] which means "complete, perfect" as opposed to partial or limited; or when applied to spiritual maturity, it means "full grown, mature, fully developed." It signifies that a purpose has been achieved. The word is used in the New Testament to signify the consummation or perfection of a process. Christ was the end or consummation of the law. He fulfilled completely and perfectly all the requirements of the law in order to make us perfect and complete before God. The man who has reached maturity, who has come of age, is *teleios*. The same Greek word is used in the following passages, translated normally in the NIV as "perfect." (Read Matthew 5:48; Matthew 19:21; Romans 12:2; 1 Corinthians 13:10; 1 Corinthians 14:20; Hebrews 9:11; James 1:17; James 1:25; 1 John 4:18)

---

24 τέλειος in the Greek.

Some conclusions about these New Testament words:

a. The concept of character, reflected in the words used, runs through-out the whole Bible. The men and women we encounter both in the Old Testament and the New Testament reveal different aspects of the char-acter of God. Christ was the fulfillment of all those character sketches we see in the Old Testament. We also see different character qualities demonstrated in the lives of the saints in the New Testament. For exam-ple, the Apostle John is known as the 'Apostle of Love'. We see both the demonstration of (for example, when John leaned on Jesus' chest and asked him a question) and teaching about love (especially in the epistles by John) running throughout his writings. In the Gospel of John we see the divinity of Christ.

b. Character and maturity are synonymous concepts in the New Testa-ment. Those who are spiritually mature are those who have Christian character.

c. One of the key concepts of character refers to that which is habitual, that which is customary for us. Indeed, when we talk about someone's character, we mean what the person habitually does.

d. Christ is the end of all perfection. He is the perfect sacrifice, who takes away our sins and brings reconciliation between sinful man and God. His character is also all perfection; He is the perfect man, the one to be emulated; He is also the end, the fulfillment of the law.

e. The whole body of Christ is maturing together, becoming more like Christ, as each part does its work.

f. We have not as yet arrived. We are all in the process of maturity.

Synonyms used in the Bible to refer to character

There are also many synonyms in the Bible, both in the Old and the New Testaments, which refer to Christian character, words like spiritual maturity, Christlikeness, or righteousness. Those who possess Christian character are referred to as the wise, the sanctified, and the holy; they have character that resembles God's character and reflects His image. "And we all, who with unveiled faces contemplate the Lord's glory, are being transformed into his image with ever-increasing glory, which comes from the Lord, who is the Spirit." (2 Corinthians 3:18) If we are being transformed into his likeness, then we come to resemble God in every way—in worldview, attitudes, values, thoughts, and behavior.

Let's look at these aspects of Christian character in more detail.

Christlikeness: The Greek word translated "exact representation" in Hebrew 1:3 is *karakter*,[25] from which the English word "character" is derived. It is used of an engraver or engraving tool, and in the New Testament, of Christ in His relation to God.

- "The Son is the radiance of God's glory and the <u>exact representation</u> of his being, sustaining all things by his powerful word. After he had provided purification for sins, he sat down at the right hand of the Majesty in heaven." (Hebrews 1:3)
- "The god of this age has blinded the minds of unbelievers, so that they cannot see the light of the gospel of the glory of Christ, who is the <u>image</u> of God." (2 Corinthians 4:4)
- "And we know that in all things God works for the good of those who love him, who have been called according to his purpose. For those God foreknew he also predestined to be conformed to the <u>likeness</u> of his Son, that he might be the firstborn among many brothers." (Romans 8:28-29)

Because Christ was God in the flesh, He exemplified and demonstrated what the character of God is like. Christlikeness, then, is Godlikeness in Christian character. The Christian walks with Jesus to learn from Jesus how to be like Jesus.[26] (Read also John 14:8; Acts 4:13; Ephesians 4:22; I Peter 1:4-7)

Righteousness: That which is "right" or "righteous" is that behavior which *ought* to happen, what *ought* to be. The word used for "righteous"

---

25 χαρακτὴρ in the Greek
26 Dallas Willard's definition of the process of discipleship.

in the OT is *saddiq*[27], used 197 times in the Bible. The Hebrew root connotes conformity to an ethical or moral standard.[28] This standard is God's nature and essence. Everything which God does is righteous because He is righteous (His nature is nothing but righteous) and cannot deviate from being righteous. Righteousness is not some quality separate from God, as though God could become righteous or more righteous, but is the essence of who God is. God doesn't act righteously because He is conforming to some external standard. He is righteous and acts righteously because He cannot deny who He is. Righteousness and judgment are the habitation of God's throne (they always characterize his actions).[29] The Bible, especially the Old Testament, gives the definition or characteristics of the righteous. They give generously[30], speak wisdom[31] and nourish many[32], praise the name of the Lord[33], know what is fitting[34]; their fruit is a tree of life[35]; their plans are just[36]; they hate what is false[37]; they leave an inheritance for their grandchildren[38]; they lead a blameless life[39]; they are bold as a lion[40]; they care about justice for the poor[41]; they detest the dishonest[42]; they walk in the righteous ways of the Lord.[43] The Greek word translated "righteous" is *dikaios*, which was a word used to refer to model citizens in the Greco-Roman world. Thus, these people were upright, just, righteous, law-abiding, honest,

---

27 צַדִּיק in the Hebrew.
28 TWOT, article on צָדֵק, vol 2, pp 752-755, article by Harold G. Stigers.
29 Ibid, p. 754.
30 Psalm 37:21; Proverbs 21:26
31 Psalm 37:30; Proverbs 10:31
32 Proverbs 10:21
33 Psalm 140:13
34 Proverbs 10:32
35 Proverbs 11:30
36 Proverbs 12:5
37 Proverbs 13:5
38 Proverbs 13:22
39 Proverbs 20:7
40 Proverbs 28:1
41 Proverbs 29:7
42 Proverbs 29:27
43 Hosea 14:9

good, just, fair, and innocent.[44] In the New Testament, righteousness is imputed by faith in Jesus Christ, who is the Righteous One. The key component of salvation in Christ is that we are declared righteous before God through the work of Christ on the cross. Christ is our righteousness, salvation, and redemption.

The wise: The Old Testament concept of *hokmâh*[45] or wisdom covers the whole gamut of human experience: wisdom in technical work, craftsmanship, execution of battle tactics, administrative skill, shrewdness in conducting our lives and prudence. The source of all wisdom is the personal God who is holy, righteous, and just.[46] Wisdom is a divine attribute, exemplified in the Messiah. Hebrew wisdom was not theoretical and speculative, as some of the wisdom literature in the ancient near east, but was based on revealed principles of right and wrong, to be lived out in daily life. Wisdom was the "perfect blend of the revealed will of a holy God with the practical human experiences of life."[47]

The sanctified: Theologian Louis Berkhof defines sanctification as "that gracious and continuous operation of the Holy Spirit, by which He delivers the justified sinner from the pollution of sin, renews his whole nature in the image of God, and enables him to perform good works."[48] The Greek word "sanctify" or "sanctified" is *hagiazo*[49], which is used to refer to things set apart for sacred purposes. It can also mean consecrated, dedicated, set apart for a holy purpose, or purified.

The holy: The concept of holiness comes from the Old Testament ceremonial system. That which was holy was that which was separated unto God. The unclean and the holy are two states which must never come in contact with each other. The only way that we can approach

44 *BibleWorks* on δίκαιος, Gingrich Lexicon.
45 חָכְמָה in the Hebrew.
46 TWOT, article on חָכְמָה (hakmah), by Louis Goldberg, Vol I, pp. 282-284.
47 Ibid, p. 283.
48 *Systematic Theology*, L. Berkhof, Wm. B. Eerdmans Publishing Co, Grand Rapids, MI, 1941, p. 532.
49 ἁγιάζω in the Greek.

God is that the sin which has separated us from God is cleansed, and the only way that we can be cleansed is through the shedding of blood. When Christ died on the cross, He was the perfect sacrifice, offered once for the forgiveness of sin so that we, those who trust in Him, can be made holy. When we receive Christ, we are declared righteous and holy; we are justified by His blood. Positionally, we are justified and holy before God.

As I mentioned at the beginning of this chapter, we really begin to understand Christian character when we see it in other people's lives. I have a good friend, whom I will call John. I have known John for about 25 years, and we served in the same church for 14 of those years. So, I know him very well. Furthermore, we are prayer partners, so we know even the issues which we both deal with on a regular basis. John is one of the most patient people whom I have ever known. He is very good at fixing computer problems and I have seen him spend hours laboring over a particular software glitch. The reason that I am not so good with fixing computer problems is that I get impatient very quickly. I am not willing to take the time to find out why my computer does what it does. But, not John. John is also a person of helps. He is always willing to drop whatever he is doing and help someone else out, whether they need a ride somewhere, or they have a plumbing problem, or they need a babysitter, or they need someone to talk to. I have learned a great deal about patience and helping other people through observing John's life. I will never be like John, but I have learned something about the character of Christ through seeing John's life up close and personal.

The distinction between discipleship and spiritual maturity

Philosopher Dallas Willard describes a disciple as "one who walks with Jesus to learn from Jesus how to be like Jesus." The word "disciple" translates from the Greek word *mathetes*[50] which means "a learner." The Greek noun comes from the verb *manthano*, which means "to learn."

---

50 μαθητής in the Greek.

Our English word derives from the Latin word *discipulus,* which means a scholar or an apprentice. It means one who directs his mind to something as a learner, disciple, or pupil, or one who attaches himself to a spiritual leader; or who adheres intellectually and spiritually to religious leaders such as Jesus. In all cases, it implies that the person not only accepts the views of the teacher, but that he is also in practice an adherent. A disciple, then, is a disciplined learner.

A disciple is someone who is in the process of learning from a master. Learning in the New Testament model is no mere intellectual process by which one acquires teaching about Christ. It implies acceptance of Christ Himself, rejection of our old existence, and the beginning a new life of discipleship in Him. It encompasses every area of life: our motivations, our attitudes, our worldview, our values, and our actions. A disciple is not necessarily a mature believer, since the word is used of a learner at any stage of the learning process. Jesus called his followers "disciples" at the beginning of His ministry with them. Thus, a disciple is not necessarily spiritually mature and does not necessarily exhibit Christian character—so Christian character and discipleship cannot be used interchangeably. Spiritual maturity and Christian character, however, can be used interchangeably.

Vital conclusions

The concept of character runs through the whole Bible, from creation through the second coming of Christ. Three vital conclusions we can draw from our deeper look at the Bible and its revelation of God's character are:

1. The whole concept of Christian character involves restored relationships. As we have said before, implicit in *shalom* is the idea of unimpaired relationships with others, and the whole concept of *shalom* includes peace with God, or an unimpaired relationship with God. Christian character involves relationships, both with God and with other people, that are restored, completed, whole, healthy, and which have integrity. It is no coincidence that when a man or woman comes to Christ that

God begins to work on restoring that person's relationships and making them whole and fulfilling. Those relationships, then, will bring fulfillment and blessing to us and to others. God wants to see our lives have fulfillment and our relationships to contribute to that fulfillment (Read John 15:12-13; Ephesians 4:32; 1 Thessalonians 5:11).

2. We can find spiritual maturity, Christian character, and completion *only* in God's presence. In the Old Testament, this completion required animal sacrifice whenever the relationship with God or others was broken. In the New Testament, the completion occurs with the blood of Christ on the cross. Only as we walk with God will we be able to have the kind of integrity, character, and lifestyle that will bring honor to Him. Christian character necessitates a lifestyle of walking with God in obedience and blessing. This is the reason why we cannot have Christian character without Christian theology and a relationship with God through Jesus Christ. We cannot have character perfection without knowing the One who is perfect (Read Romans 8:28-30).

3. We can have fullness of life and wholeness only through Jesus Christ. There is today a great emphasis on holistic ecology, holistic medicine, the benefits of a holistic lifestyle. Holistic medicine attempts to treat both the mind and the body, while holistic ecology views humans and the environment as a single system. However, if we are going to look at the whole person, we have to include man as a tripartite being: body, soul and spirit. Most importantly, we have to consider man's relationship with God as part of that wholeness. We will never have peace within, nor peace with other people unless and until we have peace with God. Holistic approaches have to include wholeness in Christ for the whole person: body, soul and spirit. God's intention is to make us whole, but only in His way through Christ (Read Ephesians 4:11-13; 1 Thessalonians 5:23).

∽

We have looked at definitions of Christian character and how it is the endpoint of the spiritually mature believer in Jesus. It is the place of peace with God, with ourselves, and with other men. Character is what God is making all of us into, while personality is the unique blend of traits which God has given to each of us. Character is also expressed and developed in and through the different roles we fulfill in life. Character is difficult to develop because our sinful nature rebels against becoming like Christ, so we are to put the sinful nature to death.

We looked at three of the Old Testament words used to express character, completeness, and maturity: *hayil, tamim* and *shalem*. We then examined some of the New Testament words used to talk about Christian character, and drew vital conclusions from those Old and New Testament words. Finally, we learned that a disciple is not necessarily a mature believer since the word is used of a learner at any stage of the learning process.

In the next chapter we will look at the process of inner transformation, being made into the image of God.

EXERCISES, QUESTIONS

1. Describe your personality. Describe your character. How do you differentiate between the two?

2. What are some of your own character strengths? What are some of your character weaknesses? (Remember, we all have weaknesses, or we would be Christ). If you can't think of any strengths and weaknesses, ask your spouse, your children, or a close friend.

3. Ask God to reveal to you one area which He wants to change into the likeness of Christ, and then ask Him to allow His Spirit to work in that area of your life.

4. Find a prayer partner with whom you can pray together on a regular basis, and commit together to work on character development.

5. Meditate on the character qualities of an elder found in 1 Timothy 3:1-7 and Titus 1:6-9.

6. Think of someone whom you consider to be spiritually mature. What are the character qualities of that person which lead you to label them as spiritually mature?

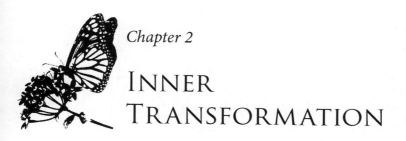

Chapter 2

Inner
Transformation

I f we are honest with ourselves, each of us realizes at some point in our lives that there is something wrong, something *missing* deep within us. We perceive we need something more. As Christians, this compels us to look at the life of Jesus and want to be more like Him. Yet when we try to imitate Him, we fall far short.

We will not have Christian character without a work of the Holy Spirit in our lives. The good news is that God has predetermined that we can become more like Christ, but only through the ongoing process He calls inner transformation. One of the greatest examples from the Bible of God's ability to change a person from the inside out is Peter. Take a look at this timeless account from Matthew 14:22-33. It is late afternoon at the Sea of Galilee when the story begins.

> We can become like Christ, but it's only through the ongoing process of inner transformation.

"Immediately Jesus made the disciples get into the boat and go on ahead of him to the other side, while he dismissed the crowd. After he had dismissed them, he went up on a mountainside by himself to pray. Later that night, he was there alone, and the boat was already a considerable distance from land, buffeted by the waves because the wind was against it. Shortly before dawn Jesus went out to them, walking on the lake. When the disciples saw him walking on the lake, they were terrified. 'It's a ghost,' they said, and cried out in fear. But

Jesus immediately said to them: 'Take courage! It is I. Don't be afraid.' 'Lord, if it's you,' Peter replied, 'tell me to come to you on the water.' 'Come,' he said. Then Peter got down out of the boat, walked on the water and came toward Jesus. But when he saw the wind, he was afraid and, beginning to sink, cried out, 'Lord, save me!' Immediately Jesus reached out his hand and caught him. 'You of little faith,' he said, 'why did you doubt?' And when they climbed into the boat, the wind died down. Then those who were in the boat worshiped him, saying, 'Truly you are the Son of God.'"

Peter was the only disciple willing to get out of the boat. Yes, he sank, but Peter was ready to take risk, a quality of a leader. He was also self-confident, believing that he could do anything. So it's not surprising that Peter took a leadership role with the disciples. His inner transformation was a work in progress. In a later scene, Jesus asks His disciples, "Who do people say that I am?" Peter isn't the first to respond, but he is the most accurate:

"Simon Peter answered, 'You are the Messiah, the Son of the living God.' Jesus replied, 'Blessed are you, Simon son of Jonah, for this was not revealed to you by flesh and blood, but by my Father in heaven. And I tell you that you are Peter, and on this rock I will build my church, and the gates of Hades will not overcome it. I will give you the keys of the kingdom of heaven; whatever you bind on earth will be bound in heaven, and whatever you loose on earth will be loosed in heaven.'" (Matthew 16:16-19) Wow! Peter nailed it, and Christ commended him and affirmed his place of leadership. Then the account continues:

"From that time on Jesus began to explain to his disciples that he must go to Jerusalem and suffer many things at the hands of the elders, the chief priests and the teachers of the law, and that he must be killed and on the third day be raised to life. Peter took him aside and began to rebuke him. 'Never, Lord!' he said. 'This shall never happen to you!' Jesus turned and said to Peter, 'Get behind me, Satan! You are a stumbling block to me; you do not have in mind the concerns of God, but merely human concerns.'" (Matthew 16:21-23)

Peter was impetuous. Not long after giving the right answer that Jesus was the Messiah, he was compelled to disagree with Jesus—and got it all wrong! Even worse, Jesus said Peter's response came from Satan himself. Peter actually thought he could prevent Jesus from going through what God had planned for Him. Later, at the advent of Jesus' suffering, Peter disowned Christ three times. Peter had to be broken of his self-confidence and self-sufficiency in order to become the type of leader God could trust with the message of salvation. Peter also had to learn that God's leader needed to get his direction from God, not from his own thinking, and that God's concept of leadership was completely different from Peter's idea of leadership.

Peter had to be transformed from the inside out. His self-confidence had to become God-confidence. Jesus loved Peter and allowed the Holy Spirit to lead him into situations through which ongoing inner transformation took place.

Inner Transformation

One of the purposes of the New Testament is to communicate that we cannot make ourselves better people. Christ died to become our redeemer, to take away our sin, and to give us a new nature which is created to be like God in righteousness and holiness—and to experience inner transformation. Human effort is not enough to live a Christian life. Inner transformation is needed.

Novelist and Christian apologist C.S. Lewis asked: "If Christianity is true why are not all Christians obviously nicer than all non-Christians? 'Niceness'—wholesome, integrated personality—is an excellent thing ... But we must not suppose that even if we succeeded in making everyone nice we should have saved their souls. A world of nice people, content in their own niceness, looking no further, turned away from God, would be just as desperately in need of salvation as a miserable world—and might even be more difficult to save." He concludes: "For mere improvement is no redemption, though redemption always improves people even here and now and will, in the end, improve them to a degree we cannot yet imagine. God became man to turn creatures into sons: not simply to produce better men of the old kind but to produce a new kind of man."[1]

Better men of the old kind are those who try harder, who may be nice people, and may be improving, but are not transformed. They do not have a new nature, do not have a relationship with Christ, are not redeemed, and are not sons of God. Those who are redeemed have been metamorphized into new creatures.

Inner transformation was predicted in the Old Testament. Jeremiah 31:33 says, "'This is the covenant I will make with the people of Israel after that time,' declares the LORD. 'I will put my law in their minds and write it on their hearts. I will be their God, and they will be my people.'" Jeremiah prophesied that there would be a new covenant which would deal with an inner work in the heart of man—but this becomes a reality with Jesus. There are only four verses in the New Testament which use the word "transform" (*metamorphow*).[2] Two of them refer to Christ's transformation before three of His disciples. The other two are these passages.

- "Therefore, I urge you, brothers and sisters, in view of God's mercy, to offer your bodies as a living sacrifice, holy and pleasing to God—this is your true and proper worship. Do not conform to the pattern of this world, but be transformed by the renewing of your mind. Then you will be able to test and approve what God's will is—his good, pleasing and perfect will." (Romans 12:1-2)
- "Now the Lord is the Spirit, and where the Spirit of the Lord is, there is freedom. And we all, who with unveiled faces contemplate the Lord's glory, are being transformed into his image with ever-increasing glory, which comes from the Lord, who is the Spirit." (2 Corinthians 3:17-18)

---

1 C.S. Lewis, *Mere Christianity*, Chapter 10, "Nice People or New Men" Collier Books, Macmillan Publishing Company, New York, NY, 1952, pp. 175-183.

2 μεταμορφοῦσθε in the Greek in Romans 12:2.

The word in the Greek in Romans 12:2 for "do not conform" is *syschymatizesthe*[3] which means "the act of an individual assuming an outward expression that does not come from within him, nor is it representative of his inner heart life."[4] The Greek is a compound word meaning formed together with, to be formed like, or be conformed to. Therefore, the pattern of this world is not representative of what we have in our inner being as a regenerated child of God. When we, as Christians, conform to the pattern of this world (mannerisms, speech expressions, styles, and habits), it is an unnatural act. We have been recreated in the image of Christ. When we assume an outward expression which doesn't come from within us, we are denying the reality of the change which has occurred as a result of the new nature within us.

Metamorphow means "the act of a person changing his outward expression from that which he has to a different one, an expression which comes from and is representative of his inner being."[5] We get our word "metamorphosis" from this Greek word. 2 Corinthians 3:18 uses the same verb, but uses the indicative voice instead of the imperative. The concept is the same: transformation from the inside out as we yield to God and allow His Holy Spirit to control our lives. Both verbs in Romans 12:2 (conform and transform) are present imperatives, meaning that the action of both verbs is ongoing. It

> Christians are not just better people. We are transformed people.

means, then, "stop allowing yourselves to be conformed... continue to let yourselves be transformed." The process has to continue repeatedly.

Consider a caterpillar and a butterfly. They are completely different. When the caterpillar goes into the cocoon, he comes out a transformed being, a process we call metamorphosis. There is a fundamental change in substance, a profound and complete change. We, as Christians, are not just better people, we are transformed people. Something has happened on the inside which affects everything, including the outside. We are brand new people, a new self.

---

3 συσχηματίζεσθε in the Greek.
4 Wuest, vol. 1, p. 206.
5 Ibid., p. 207.

Change has to take place from the inside out. Conformity takes place from the outside in but genuine, lasting change in our Christian life begins on the inside of our being. The inner man *ton esw anthropon*[6] is where God touches us at the deepest level, in our heart, our soul, our inner being. This change affects the rest of who we are.

- "For in my inner being I delight in God's law." (Romans 7:22)
- "I pray that out of his glorious riches he may strengthen you with power through his Spirit in your inner being." (Ephesians 3:16)
- "All this is for your benefit, so that the grace that is reaching more and more people may cause thanksgiving to overflow to the glory of God. Therefore we do not lose heart. Though outwardly we are wasting away, yet inwardly we are being renewed day by day." (2 Corinthians 4:15-16)
- Read also Romans 2:8-9 and 1 Peter 4:4

Outward conformity will result naturally after inward transformation has taken place. Theologian and teacher Wayne Grudem says that "as Christians grow in maturity, the kinds of sin that remain in their lives are often not so much sins of words or deeds that are outwardly noticeable to others, but inward sins of attitudes and motives of the heart."[7] Inner transformation begins with unconscious thoughts, values, worldview, and attitudes. It begins with that which is deep inside, much of which we are not even aware of.

A woman we know was sexually abused by her father, a well-known businessman in the community, when she was a child. She was abused by the same person who should have been her advocate and protector. Her mother, who suspected the problem, refused to confront her husband, preferring to maintain a façade of respectability in the community. This woman has struggled with her Christian faith and her self-image all her life. She is now getting the healing which she needs. Deep issues need

---

6   τὸν ἔσω ἄνθρωπον in the Greek.
7   Grudem, p. 752.

deep healing. We have to take care of the roots in our inner man as we are transformed with ever-increasing glory. The good news is that many people have been healed in the inner man as they have walked with Christ. The good news is that God can and will change us from the inside out.

As those who are being transformed, we often don't appreciate the incredible depth of the change which is taking place. We look the same on the outside (although our countenance will probably change) and retain the same personality and the same history. But on the inside, a revolution is underway. Theologian C. B. Cranfield, in his commentary on Romans, puts it this way: "Instead of going on contentedly and complacently allowing himself to be stamped afresh and molded by the fashion of this world, he is now to yield himself to a different pressure, to the direction of the Spirit of God. He is to allow himself to be transformed continually, remolded, remade, so that his life here and now may more and more clearly exhibit signs and tokens of the coming order of God, that order which has already come—in Christ."[8]

Thomas Brooks, a Puritan pastor who lived from 1608-1680, wrote, "I am His by purchase and I am His by conquest. I am His by donation and I am His by election. I am His by covenant and I am His by marriage; I am wholly His. I am peculiarly His, I am Universally His; I am eternally His; Once I was a slave, but now I am a son/daughter; Once I was dead but now I am alive; Once I was a child of wrath, an heir of hell but now I am a heir of Heaven; Once I was Satan's bond-servant but now I am God's freeman. Once I was under the spirit of bondage But now I am under the Spirit of adoption that seals up to me the remission of my sins, the justification of My person and the Salvation of my Soul."[9] (Read also Ephesians 4:22-24; Colossians 3:8-10; 1 Peter 1:3; 1 Peter 2:9-10)

Through inner transformation, our standing with God changes from enmity and rebellion to having received mercy; from being a stranger to a position of being a son; from a place of bearing our sin to having our sins forgiven and being redeemed from the consequences of our sin. We

---

8 Cranfield, p. 608.

9 Thomas Brooks, this quote is a compilation of two quotes from his "Epistle to the Saints." One is at location 5331, the other at location 6042 in the book *The Classic Works of Thomas Brooks.*

are born again, born from above, with God's Holy Spirit dwelling within us and sealing us for the day of redemption. We are a new creation on the inside and we have the ability to refuse the dictates of our sinful nature. We are different creatures (sons of God) with a different home (heaven), different motives (love), a different heart (a new nature), and a different family (the people of God).

A great danger is that if we have not understood that only the grace of God can and will deliver us from sin, we will merely think of Christian behavior as a product of our own effort. Inner transformation comes not from human effort, neither from our lineage, nor from educational achievement. It is a by-product of our relationship with God. God did not save us so that we could display our character as a trophy of our holiness and righteousness. The beginning place of inner transformation is a grasp with all of our being of the grace and love of God. If we have not understood that we are sinners who are in need of redemption and that only the grace of God can and will deliver us from sin, we will merely add Christian character onto our résumé. The motivation for inner transformation has to be a response in love for what God has done and for the wonderful calling which He has given us. Any other motivation will stunt our growth. Change, transformation is an outworking of an inner grace.

In his book "The Prodigal God," Timothy Keller says about the Pharisees, "The Pharisees had not been transformed, but sought only and were content with outward conformity to religious rules and practices... How can the inner workings of the heart be changed from a dynamic of fear and anger to that of love, joy, and gratitude? Here is how. You need to be moved by the sight of what it cost to bring you home. The key difference between a Pharisee and a believer in Jesus is inner-heart motivation. Pharisees are being good but out of a fear-fueled need to control God. They don't really trust him or love him. To them God is an exacting boss, not a loving father. Christians have seen something that has transformed their hearts toward God so they can finally love and rest in the Father."[10] (Read Galatians 2:20-21)

As we are being transformed from the inside out, we naturally respond

---

10 Keller, location 757.

to the grace of God with a greater love for God and a greater love for other people. Since love is the heart of God, we come to resemble Him as He changes us. As believers in Jesus Christ, we have a special place in the heart of God. We respond to that favor bestowed by grace with a return of that love to the Lord and to others, which transforms us from the inside out. Change is an outworking of an inner grace. Christian character is a response to the one who loved us, chose us, blessed us, and called us as His treasured possession. We adore God not to gain his favor, but because adoration is our response to his grace.[11] What the prophet Zephaniah said of Israel can be said of God's attitude toward us as His people: "The Lord your God is with you, the Mighty Warrior who saves. He will take great delight in you; in his love he will no longer rebuke you, but will rejoice over you with singing." (Zephaniah 3:17) Recognizing His wonderful nature and character, we respond with worship (Romans 12:2), which leads to transformation, which leads to further worship.

Character Profile
Moses - Closeness with God

Moses was born a Hebrew to a Levite woman. The Pharaoh of the land of Egypt had issued a decree to the midwives that any of the boys who were born to one of the Hebrew women should be killed at birth. Moses' parents decided to hide him instead of allowing him to be killed. When they could no longer hide him safely, they put him in a basket by the Nile. Pharaoh's daughter opened the basket, saw the baby, and took Moses home to raise as her own son. When Moses was grown up, he killed an Egyptian who was beating one of his own people, a Hebrew. Moses had to flee to Midian to avoid getting killed himself. He married a Midianite woman and tended his father-in-law's flocks. One day when Moses was eighty years old, he saw a burning bush. When he approached the bush, God spoke to Him from the bush and revealed Himself

---

11 Ibid, 96.

as the "I AM." God called Moses to return to Egypt and free the Israelites from their slavery. Moses led the Israelites in the wilderness for forty years. Moses was a great leader, but he was able to lead because he walked closely with God. The book of Exodus says that "the Lord would speak to Moses face to face, as a man speaks to a friend." (Exodus 33:11)

Christian character is developed when we are face to face with the Lord. God's presence is what transforms our character. When we behold Him, it does two things to us. First, we realize that we are in a safe place, that we can trust God, and that He loves us unconditionally. We realize that His love is overwhelming and forgiving, and that He is on our side. Second, we learn about Him, we fall in love with Him, and His character becomes both the model for transformation and the motivation for change.

The image of Christ

"Therefore, since we have such a hope, we are very bold. We are not like Moses, who would put a veil over his face to prevent the Israelites from seeing the end of what was passing away. But their minds were made dull, for to this day the same veil remains when the old covenant is read. It has not been removed, because only in Christ is it taken away. Even to this day when Moses is read, a veil covers their hearts. But whenever anyone turns to the Lord, the veil is taken away. Now the Lord is the Spirit, and where the Spirit of the Lord is, there is freedom. And we all, who with unveiled faces contemplate the Lord's glory, are being transformed into his image with ever-increasing glory, which comes from the Lord, who is the Spirit." (2 Corinthians 3:12-18)

The goal of Christian character is that we come to resemble God and His glory. Moses' glory was fading, but we are being transformed into God's likeness with a glory that is becoming stronger in us. The word used here for "into his likeness" is *eikona*[12] which means "the image

---

12 εἰκόνα in the Greek.

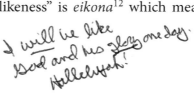
I will be like God and His glory one day. Hallelujah!

of the Son of God, into which true Christians are transformed, [the] likeness not only to the heavenly body, but also to the most holy and blessed state of mind, which Christ possesses."[13] It is the same Greek word used in Romans 8:29, Colossians 1:15, and Colossians 3:9-10. It is predetermined that we will be like Christ in the inner man—and the best news is that the image of Christ is glorious, majestic, wonderful, beyond comprehension, reflecting the image of Heaven.

So we are coming to resemble that which is heavenly as opposed to that which is earthly. Increasingly, we are coming to reflect His beauty, wholeness, truth, nobility, justice, purity, and loveliness (Philippians 4:8). We are being brought back to the place of original righteousness, which mankind had with the Father before the advent of sin. The more that we become like Him, the more His glory will be manifested in our lives. The nature of darkness is that we cannot see our way. We are stumbling our way back to the place of original righteousness. That is why it is so important that we are led by the Spirit (Galatians 5:18), live by the Spirit (Galatians 5:16), and keep in step with the Spirit (Galatians 5:25). That is why we are called to follow the person of Jesus Christ, not to try harder or follow a set of principles or rules.

> Christian character is God's glory manifested through us.

"For God, who said, 'Let light shine out of darkness,' made his light shine in our hearts to give us the light of the knowledge of God's glory displayed in the face of Christ. But we have this treasure in jars of clay to show that this all-surpassing power is from God and not from us." (2 Corinthians 4:6-7) The wonder here is that God will put His glory into human beings (jars of clay). We are nothing, yet God's glory is manifested in us and through us to the rest of the world. Christian character is God's glory manifested through us.

As we come to resemble Christ, we become in our whole being who we really are on the inside, a new creation. Our lives become integrated and we experience wholeness, integrity, harmony, and the

---

13 *BibleWorks* 9.0 on εἰκών, Thayer's Lexicon.

fruit of the Spirit. The inside and the outside of our being (our conscious and our unconscious life) come into harmony, and our thought, emotional, and physical lives gradually become integrated and whole. We are no longer merely trying to conform to Christian norms, but we become what Christ intended us to become. Jesus said, "I have come that they may have life." (John 10:10) We have been "blessed in the heavenly realms with every spiritual blessing in Christ." (Ephesians 1:3) All of these blessings come from the process of transformation in our inner being.

An erroneous approach to inner transformation: the Pharisees

American evangelist and publisher D. L. Moody told the story of an artist who wanted to paint a picture of the Prodigal Son (Luke 15:11-32). The artist searched through the madhouses, the poorhouses, and the prisons to find a man wretched enough to represent the prodigal, but he couldn't find one. Then he walked down the street one day and met a man he thought would do. He told the poor beggar he'd pay him well if he came to his room and sat for the portrait. The beggar agreed, and the day was scheduled.

"You made an appointment with me," the beggar told the artist when he was shown into the studio. The artist looked at him. "I never saw you before," he said. "You cannot have an appointment with me."

"Yes," he said. "I agreed to meet you today at ten o'clock."

"You must be mistaken; it must have been some other artist. I was to see a beggar here at this hour."

"Well," the beggar explained, "I thought I would dress myself up a bit before I got painted."

"Then I do not want you," replied the artist. "I wanted you as you were: now, you are no use to me."[14]

Jesus wants us to come to Him just as we are. He doesn't want us to get cleaned up in order to appear clean before Him. He wants to do the

---

14 Tan, P. L., selection 5399.

cleaning up Himself. Billy Graham ended his evangelism crusades with the singing of the hymn, "Just As I Am." Jesus came to call sinners, not the righteous, to repentance.

To understand the process of inner transformation, it helps to learn about the nature and role of the Pharisees and teachers of the law spoken of in the New Testament, particularly in the books of Matthew, Mark, Luke, and John. The Pharisees formed closed communities with strict rules for admission where the person desiring admittance had to prove his ability to keep the ritual Mosaic law. While the scribes were the educated religious zealots, Pharisees were common people, men with little or no scribal education who were earnest and self-sacrificing. All too often, though, they were not free from being uncharitable and acting with pride toward the masses. Why? They considered themselves to be the true Israel and wanted to build up a universal priesthood. As such, people looked to them as models of voluntary commitment to piety.

American Christian author Philip Yancey said of the Pharisees, "God's law [the Old Testament] contains 248 commandments and 365 prohibitions, and they were determined to keep them all. They also had 1,521 additions to the list. For example, in order to fulfill the third commandment, 'You shall not misuse the name of the Lord,' they refused to pronounce God's name at all. To avoid sexual temptation, they had a practice of lowering their heads and not even looking at women (the most scrupulous of these were known as 'bleeding Pharisees' because of frequent collisions with walls and other obstacles). To avoid defiling the Sabbath, they outlawed thirty-nine activities that might be construed as 'work.' It must have been quite a blow when Jesus said that these pious and popular individuals could not even get into the Kingdom of God, let alone enjoy a special status in the Kingdom."

Yancey continues: "The Pharisees were very strict. How can we exceed their righteousness? They were meticulous in keeping the law. Our righteousness has to exceed that of the Pharisees not in degree, but in kind. Our righteousness has to be a different kind of righteousness. It is not that the Christian can keep 240 of the commandments and that the Pharisees could only keep 230. No, Christian righteousness exceeds that of the

Pharisees because it is a righteousness of the heart. It is deeper, internal, rather than shallow and external."[15]

Indeed, Jesus had the most trouble with the Pharisees. Timothy Keller compared the Pharisees with the elder brother in the biblical parable in Luke 15:11-32. The elder brother served the father and never disobeyed his father's orders. He was religious, but not transformed. The elder brother illustrates the way of moral conformity. The moral conformist believes that the people who do their own thing are the problem with the world, and moral people are the solution. Likewise, the Pharisees had religion but not relationship; they followed rules made by men, not the rules laid down by the Lord. They were good people, but not transformed people. Keller wrote:

"Underneath the brothers' [the younger brother who spent all his inheritance and the elder brother who remained at home] sharply different patterns of behavior is the same motivation and aim. Both are using the father in different ways to get the things on which their hearts are really fixed. It was the wealth, not the love of the father, that they believed would make them happy and fulfilled. At the end of the story, the elder brother has an opportunity to truly delight the father by going into the feast. But his resentful refusal shows that the father's happiness had never been his goal.[16] There are two ways to be your own Savior and Lord. One is by breaking all the moral laws and setting your own course, and one is keeping all the moral laws and being very, very good.[17] Elder brothers divide the world in two: 'The good people (like us) are in and the bad people, who are the real problem with the world, are out.' Younger brothers, even if they don't believe in God at all, do the same thing, saying, 'No, the open-minded and tolerant people, who are the real problem with the world are out.' But Jesus says, 'The humble are in and the proud are out.'"[18]

Jesus said: "Woe to you, teachers of the law and Pharisees, you hypocrites! You give a tenth of your spices—mint, dill and cumin. But you

---

15 Yancey, *The Jesus I Never Knew*, p. 132.
16 Keller, location 373.
17 Keller, location, 415.
18 Ibid, location 426.

have neglected the more important matters of the law—justice, mercy and faithfulness. You should have practiced the latter, without neglecting the former." (Matthew 23:23) What were the problems with the Pharisees? Their obedience was only external. They did what they did so that men would see. They had not dealt with their motives, but only with actions. Thus, their motives for keeping the law were not right. There was no inner transformation, but only outward conformity to external rules.

Religion is not enough. We have to have a heart relationship with the God of the universe through Jesus Christ. Piety has to be inward. Keeping rules is much easier than following Jesus. It is much easier not to murder than to deal with lust in your heart. It is much easier not to tell a lie than it is to deal with unforgiveness toward the person who has hurt you or your loved ones. The book of Colossians is written to talk about how we have been given fullness in Christ. He is the solution to sin. We cannot overcome our sinful nature through self-imposed discipline. Author Don Mostrom calls legalism a choice of our sinful nature, saying it is much easier to give up what we want to give up than to lay everything down for Jesus' sake. If we follow rules and regulations instead of Christ, he adds, we can make up our own rules and feel very good when we keep them. Legalism can help us to feel good about ourselves, but it does nothing to enable us to follow Jesus.[19]

> Religion is not enough. We have to have a heart relationship with the God of the universe through Jesus Christ.

"So then, just as you received Christ Jesus as Lord, continue to live your lives in him, rooted and built up in him, strengthened in the faith as you were taught, and overflowing with thankfulness. See to it that no one takes you captive through hollow and deceptive philosophy, which depends on human tradition and the elemental spiritual forces of this world rather than on Christ. For in Christ all the fullness of the Deity lives in bodily form, and in Christ you have been brought to fullness. He is the head over every power and authority." (Colossians 2:6-10)

---

19 Paraphrased from Mostrom's book entitled *Spiritual Privileges You Didn't Know Were Yours.*

The Pharisees also failed because they concentrated on keeping traditions of men rather than the commands of God. The problem with keeping religious rules and regulations is that if we keep them, we get proud. If we don't keep them, we get condemned. Jesus came to free us from pride and condemnation. In addition, the Pharisees treated all the requirements of the Law on the same level. They tended to major on the minors and minor on the majors. I have a friend who was a member of a very legalistic congregation for many years, and was the choir director in her church. One of the requirements in the church was that women in ministry could never cut their hair. When she cut her hair she was fired from her position. She and her husband left the church. This church majored on the minors (women not cutting their hair) and minored on the majors (love). The emphasis in the church was on outward appearance and the keeping of rules, not on things such as mercy, love, holiness, and integrity.

Character Profile
Paul - Recognition of the Grace of God

The apostle Paul was originally Saul, a Pharisaic zealot who wanted to do all he could to oppose the Christians who were in Jerusalem. When they were put to death, he cast his lot in favor of seeing them martyred for their faith (Acts 26:9-10). He called himself the worst of sinners (1 Timothy 1:15) and he realized that God had forgiven him to demonstrate His overwhelming grace. God called him to a special ministry of proclaiming that grace to the Gentiles. Paul wrote many letters which are now part of the New Testament and he stood against those who tried to make the Gentiles keep the Mosaic law in order to be saved. He even withstood Peter when he would not eat with the Gentiles after some other believers came from Jerusalem to Antioch. Paul understood the great cost of abandoning a complete reliance on God's grace.

Our faith is built on the foundation of the grace of God. We are saved by grace alone through faith (Ephesians 2:8). If we believe that we are saved through any merit of our own, we will attempt to please God through human traditions and false humility (Colossians 2:18). Nothing but God's pure love for us and the sacrifice of His son on the cross contributed to our acceptance by the Father. Paul understood this and based his life on God's acceptance of him through grace. Christian character has to be established on grace and grace alone.

Finally, the Pharisees did not practice what they preached because they couldn't possibly keep all the laws. Furthermore, they weren't motivated to help people, but were focused on their own righteousness rather than on others. Jesus told others not to do what the Pharisees do, because "they tie up heavy, cumbersome loads and put them on other people's shoulders, but they themselves are not willing to lift a finger to move them." (Matthew 23:4)

What is transformed thinking? The following two charts illustrate the vast difference between ungodly thinking and godly thinking. For a version in which the entire passages are spelled out, consult Appendix 1.

TRAITS OF UNGODLY THINKING

TRAIT	PASSAGES
Futile	Romans 1:21; 1 Corinthians 3:20; Ephesians 4:17
Darkened	Romans 1:21; Ephesians 4:18
Separated from the life of God	Ephesians 4:18
Hardened hearts	Romans 1:21; Ephesians 4:18
Ignorant	Ephesians 4:18
Foolish	Romans 1:22
Believe lies	Romans 1:25; John 8:44
Depraved	Romans 1:28; 2 Timothy 3:8
Minds set on what sinful nature desires	Romans 8:5
Dull	2 Corinthians 3:14

TRAIT	PASSAGES
Led astray	2 Corinthians 11:3
Enemies of God	Colossians 1:21
Set on earthly things	Colossians 3:2
Impure	Titus 1:15
Corrupted	Titus 1:15
Conforms to the pattern of this world	Romans 12:2
Leads to death	Romans 8:6
Set on what the sinful nature desires	Romans 8:5
Hostile to God	Romans 8:7
Doesn't submit to God's law	Romans 8:7
Cannot submit to God's law	Romans 8:7

TRAITS OF GODLY THINKING

TRAIT	PASSAGES
Glorify God	Romans 1:21
Give thanks to God	Romans 1:21
Wise	Matthew 7:24; 2 Timothy 3:14,15
Produce good fruit	James 3:17
Pure	James 3:17
Peace-loving	James 3:17
Considerate	James 3:17
Submissive	James 3:17
Full of mercy	James 3:17
Impartial	James 3:17
Sincere	James 3:17
Mature	1 Corinthians 14:20
Wholesome	2 Peter 3:1
Enlightened	Ephesians 1:18
Set on what the Spirit desires	Romans 8:5
Life and peace	Romans 8:6
In accord with the Truth	John 8:31,32; John 14:16,17; John 16:13 John 17:17; Romans 1:25

Paul says in Romans and 2 Corinthians that our thinking is to be transformed. Let's look at some conclusions about the traits of ungodly thinking and the contrast with Godly thinking. First, you can't have thinking which accords with truth and with a lie. There is no middle ground. We either live by the Spirit or by our sinful nature (Galatians 5:16-18). Either our sinful nature is crucified or it isn't (Galatians 5:24). We are either controlled by our sinful nature or by the Spirit of God.

Second, renewed thinking is wise, pure, peace-loving, considerate, submissive, full of mercy, impartial, sincere, mature, wholesome, enlightened, soft, produces life and peace, and is in accord with biblical truth. The renewed mind glorifies and gives thanks to God and produces good fruit. The mind which is renewed is set on what the Spirit desires.

Third, in contrast, the thinking which is not renewed is futile, darkened, depraved, separated from the life of God, comes from a hardened heart, ignorant, and foolish It is controlled by the sinful nature, dull, led astray, impure, and is an enemy of God set on earthly things that are corrupted. This type of thinking leads to spiritual death. The whole nature of this type of thinking is that it comes from deception and darkness. A depraved, dark, hardened, and ungodly mind doesn't know that it is separated from God. That is exactly why it takes a renewed mind and a new nature. We cannot think our way out of deception and darkness.

Our reasoning is insufficient to bring us to the light, because it is controlled by the sinful nature. Something has to change. Something has to come into our lives from the outside—God. Only with revelation from God's Holy Spirit living inside of us can we move from darkness to light. It takes God to turn us from caterpillars to butterflies.

Finally, there is a great contrast between the darkness and the light. Darkness and light cannot coexist. Darkness and light are mutually exclusive; we either are in spiritual darkness or we are in the light. As believers we sometimes don't realize the incredible difference between our thinking and the thinking of those who don't have a new nature. The difference is profound, moving us from the power of Satan into the Kingdom of God, where light shines.

- "For you were once darkness, but now you are light in the Lord. Live as children of light." (Ephesians 5:8)
- "For he has rescued us from the dominion of darkness and brought us into the kingdom of the Son he loves." (Colossians 1:13)

Vital conclusions

If you don't know Jesus Christ as Savior and Lord of your life, then you need to invite Him into your inner man and begin a new life with Christ in your heart. You will be only frustrated with trying to be a good person. You need a new nature in order to live a new life.

1. Don't seek conformity to this culture, nor to mere church customs and rules. Certainly, there is a culture in every church, but we should not seek to conform socially, but to be transformed spiritually. You should not seek to be a better person with a better attitude, values, and behavior, but to be a transformed person, born again and possessing a new nature which gives you new power to do what you know you should be doing. Allow God to transform you.

2. If you have been born again, realize the profound change that has taken place in your inner man. You are not just a different person, or even a better person, you are a new person. As you allow this realization to fill you with gratitude toward God, you will realize that Christ has broken the power of sin in your life. God does not want you to just "get by." He wants you to live a victorious, Christ-centered, overcoming life.

3. You still have old habits that are sometimes hard to break: negative thinking, laziness, dishonesty, lust, gossiping, or any host of other habits. As you walk with Christ and allow Him to transform you from the inside out, you'll gradually drop off those old habits and behaviors. Of course, this process takes time and willingness to change, but Christ has given you both the exhortations to change and the power to change. He doesn't ask you to do anything He hasn't given you the ability to do through His Holy Spirit.

4. If you allow inner transformation to work within you, it'll positively impact your emotions, spiritual walk, marriage, relationships in the workplace, attitudes toward money and authority, your thought life—everything. The goal is that you become like Christ and that your life increasingly reflects His glory. The good news is that this transformation is totally satisfying to the human soul. God is not trying to make you miserable. He wants to set you free.

∽

This chapter explored the process of inner transformation. It is the work of God's Holy Spirit within you through the new birth you receive when we accept Jesus. You have a new nature which is being transformed into the image of Christ. It is not effort, but relationship, which transforms you, and as you seek Christ, His Spirit does a work of recreating you into what you were designed to be from the beginning of time. This process takes place through the renewing of your mind.

We looked at the Pharisees, who missed the grace of God because they were looking at attaining righteousness through the keeping of the law. They were sincere, but their obedience was only external; their focus was on keeping the traditions of men. They treated all the requirements of the Mosaic law on the same level, and they did not practice what they preached. They were trying to be justified through self-effort instead of trusting in God for their righteousness.

Then we looked at the contrast between ungodly thinking and godly thinking. We concluded that we are incapable of arriving at righteousness through our own thought patterns, since our thinking without the Spirit, without the new nature, will not lead to the life which we and God desires. Darkness and light cannot coexist.

In the next chapter, we will look at the two primary agents God uses in the process of transforming us into the image of Christ.

EXERCISES, QUESTIONS

1. In what areas of your life are you depending on your own abilities instead of on Christ?

2. In what ways does the culture of your church promote legalism rather than enabling the people of the church to have power over the sinful nature?

3. What does Paul mean when he says in Galatians 2:20, "I have been crucified with Christ and I no longer live, but Christ lives in me. The life I live in the body, I live by faith in the Son of God, who loved me and gave himself for me?"

4. Why is it necessary for Christians to be transformed on the inside in order to be transformed on the outside? Why can't we concentrate on changing our behavior first, and then work on attitudes, motives, and worldview later?

Chapter 3

THE AGENTS OF INNER TRANSFORMATION

I have found that as I walk with Christ, He transforms me, changes me, and draws me closer to Himself. He brings me into a place of greater joy, love, freedom, and fulfillment as I journey with Him through life. This process of sanctification, performed by the two primary agents—His Word and His Spirit—operates like a gentle surgeon, cutting away the parts of my character which are destructive and bringing me into the continuous health of life in Him.

In one of Jesus' final discourses, He spoke of this process with an illustration. "I am the true vine, and my Father is the gardener. He cuts off every branch in me that bears no fruit, while every branch that does bear fruit he prunes so that it will be even more fruitful. You are already clean because of the word I have spoken to you. Remain in me, and I will remain in you. No branch can bear fruit by itself; it must remain in the vine. Neither can you bear fruit unless you remain in me. I am the vine; you are the branches. If a man remains in me and I in him, he will bear much fruit; apart from me you can do nothing." (John 15:1-5)

Sometimes the very character qualities in us which are most productive will be pruned so that they can become more fruitful. The older I get, the more I realize the depth of my own sinfulness, the greatness of His love, the sweetness of His presence, and the breadth of His goodness. I realize how much I need to walk with Him daily, trust in Him completely, and believe that whatever He does in my life is for my benefit.

His pruning is painful at times, but the end result is that I become more like Him and therefore more loving toward those who are lost in sin. Romans 8:28-29 affirms, "And we know that in all things God works for the good of those who love him, who have been called according to his purpose. For those God foreknew he also predestined to be conformed to the image of his Son, that he might be the firstborn among many brothers."

The Savoy Declaration, a modification of the Westminster Confession of Faith (1646), details the two agents of sanctification:

"They that are united to Christ, effectually called and regenerated, having a new heart and a new spirit created in them, through the virtue of Christ's death and resurrection, are also further sanctified really and personally through the same virtue, by his Word and Spirit dwelling in them; the dominion of the whole body of sin is destroyed, and the several lusts thereof are more and more weakened, and mortified, and they more and more quickened, and strengthened in all saving graces, to the practice of all true holiness, without which no man shall see the Lord." It goes on to say, "This sanctification is throughout in the whole man, yet imperfect in this life, there abideth still some remnants of corruption in every part, whence ariseth a continual and irreconcilable war, the flesh lusting against the spirit, and the spirit against the flesh … In which war, although the remaining corruption for a time may prevail, yet through the continual supply of strength from the sanctifying Spirit of Christ, the regenerate part doth overcome, and so the Saints grow in grace, perfecting holiness in the fear of God." [1]

> The Bible is inerrant and the anchor for our lives.

Agent #1: God's Word

The utter reliability of God's Word, the Bible, is stated in 2 Timothy 3:16-17. "All Scripture is God-breathed and is useful for teaching, rebuking, correcting and training in righteousness, so that the man of God may be thoroughly equipped for every good work." The Greek word translated

---

1 *Creeds and Platforms of Congregationalism*, Williston Walker, Pilgrim Press, Philadelphia, Boston, 1960.

"God-breathed" is *theopneustos*,[2] which means a communication that has been ordained by God's authority and produced by the enabling of His Spirit. It literally means "out-breathed by God."

It is vital that the Bible is understood to be inerrant and the anchor for our lives. A five-point statement from the Chicago Statement on Biblical Inerrancy (1978) reads as follows:

1. God, who is Himself truth and speaks truth only, has inspired Holy Scripture in order thereby to reveal Himself to lost mankind through Jesus Christ as Creator and Lord, Redeemer and Judge. Holy Scripture is God's witness to Himself.

2. Holy Scripture, being God's own Word, written by men prepared and superintended by His Spirit, is of infallible divine authority in all matters upon which it touches: it is to be believed, as God's instruction, in all that it affirms: obeyed, as God's command, in all that it requires; embraced, as God's pledge, in all that it promises.

3. The Holy Spirit, Scripture's divine Author, both authenticates it to us by His inward witness and opens our minds to understand its meaning.

4. Being wholly and verbally God-given, Scripture is without error or fault in all its teaching, no less in what it states about God's acts in creation, about the events of world history, and about its own literary origins under God, than in its witness to God's saving grace in individual lives.

5. The authority of Scripture is inescapably impaired if this total divine inerrancy is in any way limited or disregarded, or made relative to a view of truth contrary to the Bible's own; and such lapses bring serious loss to both the individual and the Church.[3]

---

2 θεόπνευστος in the Greek.

3 For the full statement on Biblical inerrancy, go to: http://www.bible-researcher.com

God's Word is the source of truth. Look at this trio of verses from the wisdom books of Psalms and Proverbs:

- "Show me your ways, Lord, teach me your paths; Guide me in your truth and teach me, for you are God my Savior, and my hope is in you all day long." (Psalm 25:4-5)
- "I have chosen the way of truth; I have set my heart on your laws." (Psalm 119:30)
- "Buy the truth and do not sell it—wisdom, instruction and insight as well." (Proverbs 23:23)
- Read also Psalm 43:3-4; Psalm 86:11; Zechariah 8:16-17

The Hebrew word *emet* means "firmness, truth." At the heart of the meaning of the root is the idea of certainty or dependability. It is a characteristic of the nature of God, and as a result is applied to God's words. If God is certain, then His Word is certain as well. An article in the Theological Wordbook of the Old Testament says it is "manifestly clear that there is no truth in the biblical sense, i.e. valid truth, outside God. All truth comes from God and is truth because it is related to God."

Character Profile
Abraham - Faith

Abraham is called the father of our faith. "By faith Abraham, when called to go to a place he would later receive as his inheritance, obeyed and went, even though he did not know where he was going. By faith he made his home in the promised land like a stranger in a foreign country; he lived in tents, as did Isaac and Jacob, who were heirs with him of the same promise. For he was looking forward to the city with foundations, whose architect and builder is God." (Hebrews 11:8-10) At the word and promise of God, Abraham left Ur of the Chaldeans in order to go to a land (Canaan) that he had never seen. He trusted God to give him the whole land of Canaan, which ultimately became the land of the Israelites. He left that which was familiar to go to that which was unfamiliar, but which God had promised.

There are two lessons for us here pertaining to Christian character. First, in order to pursue Christian character, we need to believe that our life on this Earth is not all that there is. Hebrews 11:10 says that Abraham was looking forward to an eternal city. We are looking forward to an eternal existence. We are looking for a better place in Heaven. In order to pursue Christian character, we have to believe God exists and that He rewards those who earnestly seek Him (Hebrews 11:6). We have to believe that God has planned something better for us (Hebrews 11:40). Second, Abraham left that which was familiar (the city of Ur) for that which was unfamiliar (the land of Canaan). It is always easier and more comfortable to stay where we are and play it safe. But we are called to something better (inner transformation) and to forsake that which is familiar (our culture, our sinful nature, and our comfort). Every step forward in our Christian life requires leaving the familiar for the unfamiliar. All we have to go on is that God is good and that He is trying to take us to a new land which is far better than anything we have known before (Ephesians 3:20).

In the New Testament, *alythys*[4] means "verity, truth." Universally it is "what is true in any matter under consideration" (as opposed to what is feigned, fictitious, false). Subjectively, it means "truth as a personal excellence; that candor of mind which is free from affectation, pretence, simulation, falsehood, deceit; sincerity of mind and integrity of character, or a mode of life in harmony with divine truth."[5] John 8:32 states, "Then you will know the truth, and the truth will set you free." (Read also John 1:14, 17, 21; John 4:24; John 15:26; John 16:13; John 17:17; Romans 1:18, 25; 1 Corinthians 13:6; Ephesians 1:13; Ephesians 4:15; Ephesians 6:14; James 1:18)

---

4 ἀληθής in the Greek.
5 BibleWorks 9.0 on ἀλήθεια, (*alytheia*) Thayer's Lexicon.

God's Word is not just ideas and theories; it is truth—that *which is* as opposed to that *which is not*. Every doctrine and every thought which does not line up with God's Word is a lie. Truth sets a standard of perfection in our lives. We learn from Scripture what character is meant to be, both through the examples given in the lives of those who have gone before us and in the exhortations to holy living which run throughout the Bible. In Hebrews 11, we read about several characters in Scripture, heroes of the Christian faith who lived according to His truth in the midst of difficulties and opposition. We have the book of Proverbs, which provides exhortations to holy living and righteousness. In the Bible, we have a clear standard. We know how we are to live, and we have God's promise that His Holy Spirit is at work in us to help us live according to His precepts.

Christ came to Earth to demonstrate through His character the nature of God. He not only taught and healed; He was the embodiment of God the Father. In John 14:8-10, Philip said, "Lord, show us the Father and that will be enough for us." Jesus answered: "Don't you know me, Philip, even after I have been among you such a long time? Anyone who has seen me has seen the Father. How can you say, 'Show us the Father'? Don't you believe that I am in the Father, and that the Father is in me? The words I say to you I do not speak on my own authority. Rather, it is the Father, living in me, who is doing his work." Jesus embodied Christian worldview, attitudes, values, motivation, and behavior. (Read also Luke 17:20; John 14:16-20, 23; Colossians 1:25-27)

Truth transcends our perceived experience. In our age, there is an incredible attack on truth. A statement that you often hear is "your truth is your truth and my truth is my truth." In other words, our experience and our perception of reality are enough. There is no transcendent truth above what we think and feel. There is no absolute truth—only relative truth. Christian Smith and Hilary Davidson's book, "Lost in Transition: The Dark Side of Emerging Adulthood," recounts the results of their decade-long study of a representative sample of Americans aged 18-23. Through in-depth interviews, they concluded that an alarming percentage of young people are highly materialistic, commitment averse, disengaged from political and civic life, sexually irresponsible, often heavily intoxicated, and morally confused. In fact, the authors contend, they lack even the vocabulary to think in moral terms. Six out of ten told the authors that morality is a "personal choice," like preferring long or short hair. One young woman, a student at an Ivy League college, explained that while she doesn't cheat, she is loath to judge others who do. A young man related how often "it changes from person to person. What you may think is right may not necessarily be right for me." American columnist and political analyst Mona Charen comments that "the irony is that this supposed reluctance to make moral judgments is itself a moral posture."[6]

D. A. Carson says that the definition of the word "tolerance" has been changed. "Under the older view of tolerance, a person might be judged tolerant if, while holding strong views, he or she insisted that others had the right to dissent from those views and argue their own cases. This view of tolerance is in line with the famous utterance often (if erroneously) assigned to Voltaire: 'I disapprove of what you say, but I will defend to the death your right to say it.'"[7] He goes on to talk about the new definition of tolerance "that there is no one view that is exclusively true. Strong opinions are nothing more than strong preferences for a particular version or reality, each version equally true ... We must be tolerant, not because we cannot distinguish the right path from the wrong path, but because all paths are equally right."

If you begin with this new view of tolerance, and then elevate this view to the supreme position in the hierarchy of moral virtues, the supreme sin is *in*tolerance. The trouble is that such intolerance, like the new tolerance, also takes on a new definition. Intolerance is no longer a refusal to allow contrary opinions to say their piece in public, but must be understood to be any questioning or contradicting the view that all opinions are equal in value, that all worldviews have equal worth, that all stances are equally valid. To question such postmodern axioms is by

---

6   Mona Charen, "Moral Abdication and Multiculturalism", *Jewish World Review*, Nov 4, 2011.
7   Carson, p. 6.

definition intolerant ... The definition of the new tolerance is that every individual's beliefs, values, lifestyle, and perception of truth claims are equal ... There is no hierarchy of truth. Your beliefs and my beliefs are equal, and all truth is relative."[8]

If there is no truth beyond what we individually think and feel, then there is no standard on which we can judge right and wrong. All standards are relative and shifting. For example, if you believe that homosexuality is acceptable, there is nothing I can point to that proves you are wrong, since your experience is what matters. You have known homosexuals and they were really nice people, so their lifestyle is perfectly acceptable—even, you believe, in the eyes of God, who doesn't judge. As long as you feel good about yourself, you are fine. But believers in Christ believe that God's Word is truth. Our character is to conform to truth. Jesus is the way, the *truth*, and the life. The truth sets us free. If there is a God and He has established truth, then we are accountable to that standard. Yet increasingly in America, we have discarded God's standard and gone our own way. The whole essence of the Bible is that God created man, and that God is calling men to account for their beliefs and actions. One day, we will all give an account to God. He is absolute. He is sovereign. He is all powerful. He is above all.

Truth is also not found in philosophy or theories, but rather in the *person* of Jesus Christ, the unique Son of God and the living embodiment of truth. Consequently, knowing truth depends on being in proper relationship to Christ, who is divine truth. Jesus spoke the truth, but He also said that He is the truth. John 14:5-7 reads: "Thomas said to him, 'Lord, we don't know where you are going, so how can we know the way?' Jesus answered, 'I am the way and the truth and the life. No one comes to the Father except through me. If you really know me, you will know my Father as well. From now on, you do know him and have seen him.'" Christ embodies all truth. He is truth in human form. Therefore, we cannot mature spiritually, emotionally, and in our character unless we are also maturing in our walk with Christ. Christian character is

---

8 Ibid., pp. 11-13.

developed in the process of walking with Christ through life, not in abstract or in theory.

To walk as Jesus walked means that we have to live in Him. We cannot say that we know Him and not live as He did. The reason that God became human flesh was to demonstrate to us that we can walk in integrity and still be a human being. Jesus walked a sinless life. He came to be a visual example of what a life of obedience looks like. Therefore, every area of our character is to be governed by and respond to truth.

> To walk as Jesus walked means that we have to live in Him.

Integrity is when God's truth penetrates into our inner man so that we reflect God's character in our relationship with Him, with others, and with ourselves. Truth grows in every part of our being, replacing lies and distortion and working to establish God's righteousness. There is nothing hidden. Every motive has been exposed to God's truth.

So, for example, I become aware that there is a deep-seated anger in my heart. I might not even be aware it is there, but it comes out, usually through interacting with other people. I go to the Bible and read the words of Jesus: "Anyone who is angry with a brother or sister will be subject to judgment." (Matthew 5:22) I then begin to pray that God will show me the root, the source of the anger. When He shows me the source, I begin to pray about that problem. Many times God will take me through a difficult situation in my life where that anger comes to the surface. I confess the anger and He deals with the root issues in my heart. One day, I find myself in a similar situation - and I find that the anger is no longer there. Truth, God's presence, has been established in that area of my life. I am amazed that, although I didn't realize that He was dealing with the problem, He was bringing healing and truth to that area of my life. The scripture is fulfilled which says "And we know that in all things God works for the good of those who love him, who have been called according to his purpose." (Romans 8:28) God has been at work when I had no clue that He was using the circumstances in my life to bring inner healing to me.

Evangelical leader John Stott says "followers of Jesus are to be different—different from both the nominal church and the secular world, different from both the religious and the irreligious. The Sermon on the Mount (Matthew 5-7) is the most complete delineation anywhere in the New Testament of the Christian counterculture. Here is a Christian value system, ethical standard, religious devotion, attitude to money, ambition, lifestyle, and network of relationships—all of which are totally at variance with those of the non-Christian world."[9]

Agent #2: God's Spirit

When Jesus was getting ready to leave the Earth, He wanted to encourage His disciples and so He introduced them to the concept of the Holy Spirit, the third person of the Trinity. He said that He would send the Holy Spirit to indwell believers. In John 16:7, Jesus said, "But very truly I tell you, it is for your good that I am going away. Unless I go away, the Advocate will not come to you; but if I go, I will send him to you." Along with God's Word the Bible, the Holy Spirit is the second agent of inner transformation in our lives. The Holy Spirit is not just an influence or a force, but a living being both personal and divine, having mind, will, and emotions.

Co-eternal in the Godhead, the Holy Spirit is called :

God[10]
eternal[11]
omnipotent
all powerful[12]
omniscient, all knowing[13]
omnipresent, everywhere-present[14]
and the source of life[15].

9 Stott, p. 19.
10 Acts 5:3-4; 1 Corinthians 3:16; I Corinthians 12:4-6
11 Hebrews 9:14
12 Luke 1:35
13 John 14:26; John 16:12-13; 1 Corinthians 2:10; Romans 8:26-27
14 Psalms 139:7-10
15 Romans 8:2

We also see in Scripture that the Spirit
  works[16]
  searches[17]
  speaks[18]
  testifies[19]
  bears witness[20]
  teaches[21]
  reproves[22]
  prays and makes intercession[23]
  leads[24]
  guides the believer into all truth[25]
  glorifies the Lord Jesus Christ[26]
  brings about regeneration[27]
  strives with people[28]
  convicts people[29]
  sends messengers from God[30]
  calls people into ministry[31]
  directs people in the service of Christ[32]
  and imparts spiritual gifts to the members of the Body of Christ[33]

---

16 1 Corinthians 12:11
17 1 Corinthians 2:10
18 Acts 13:2; Revelation 2:7; 2 Samuel 23:2; Matthew 10:20; 1 Timothy 4:1
19 John 15:26; Nehemiah 9:30
20 1 John 5:6
21 John 14:26; Nehemiah 9:20
22 John 16:8-11
23 Romans 8:26
24 Matthew 4:1
25 John 16:13
26 John 16:14
27 John 3:5-6
28 Genesis 6:3
29 John 16:8
30 Isaiah 48:16
31 Acts 13:2; Acts 20:28
32 Acts 8:29; Acts 10:19; Acts 16:6-7
33 1 Corinthians 12:7-11

It is clear that God's Spirit is at work within Christians to conform us to the image of Christ. How does God's Holy Spirit transform us?

The Holy Spirit is the comforter, the counselor, the one called alongside to help. The Holy Spirit (the Counselor) in the Greek is the word *paraklytos*[34] or "paraclete." Biblical scholar Raymond Brown gives four possible meanings of the word *paraklytos*: first, "one called alongside to help," an advocate or defense attorney; second, an "intercessor, mediator, spokesman"; third, a "comforter or consoler"; and fourth, "one who bears witness." Brown concludes, "we find that no one translation of *paraklytos* captures the complexity of the functions, forensic and otherwise, that this figure has. The Paraclete is a witness in defense of Jesus and a spokesman for him in the context of his trial by his enemies; the Paraclete is a consoler of the disciples for he takes Jesus' place among them; the Paraclete is a teacher and a guide of the disciples and thus their helper."[35] Because Christ lives in us, we have the help of the Spirit of Christ, the Counselor, to teach us all things. We are not helpless in this journey.

The Holy Spirit guides us into truth and reveals truth. The Spirit reveals truth, communicates truth, agrees with truth, and is truth. It is our sinful nature's confrontation with truth that produces repentance. If we had not known truth, we would go on in our sinfulness. The law reveals the areas in which we don't measure up to the standard. But the law itself cannot bring obedience, only knowledge of sin. God's Spirit brings healing and power to overcome the different areas of our own sinfulness.

If we could arrive at spiritual truth through natural understanding, then the Christian life would be best understood by scholars. Instead, the Christian life is understood by disciples. Only in obedience, only in living with and walking with Christ, can we learn who the Father is. If the Christian life could be achieved through greater effort, then our becoming like Christ would only occur as a result of trying harder. The most disciplined would be the most godly. Those who work harder would be the most like Christ. But it is not through effort that we are transformed, but through yielding to the Spirit of Christ within us.

PROFOUND

---

34 Παράκλητος in the Greek.
35 The Gospel According to John, *The Anchor Bible*, pp. 1136, 1137

Certainly effort is needed, and those who desire Christ are the ones who are transformed, but the effort is toward desiring Christ and yearning for Him, not toward applying principles, strategies and disciplines. (Read Galatians 3:23-25; Romans 2:14-15)

The Holy Spirit applies God's truth to our lives. The requirements of the law are written on our hearts (Jeremiah 31:31-33). The law, which is external, agrees with our conscience, which is internal. Because we are made in the image of God, our conscience, our inner man, agrees with the law. Integrity occurs when the external agrees with the internal, when what we do agrees with who we are. The Holy Spirit changes every part of us, even our unconscious motives. Our righteousness has to extend to our hidden motives, not just to our actions. As Bible teacher and author Rick Warren says, "Christlikeness is not produced by imitation, but by inhabitation."[36] That's why it is so important to be in fellowship with other believers and to be sitting under biblical teaching. Our character cannot change when we are not hearing and obeying God's Word.

> The Holy Spirit reveals God's likeness to us.

The Holy Spirit reveals God's character to us, and helps us keep in relationship with the Lord. The pattern, the model of Christian character, lives within us. Inner transformation is becoming who we really are on the inside. However, we also have a sinful nature on the inside. Thus we are exhorted not to be led by the sinful nature, but by the Spirit of Christ. We have a choice of which power to obey and follow.

The Holy Spirit reveals God's likeness to us. We cannot and will not know who God is and what He is like without revelation. Only through Christ can we know God and know what He is like. In the Old Testament, the children of Israel would not have known who God was if He had not revealed Himself to them through servants such as Noah, Abraham, Moses, David, and many others. God is still revealing Himself to us through His Spirit within us. (Read 1 Corinthians 2:9-11; John 14:8-10; Galatians 5:16, 25)

---

36 Warren, *Purpose Driven Life*, p. 174.

The Holy Spirit leads us and fills us. Because the Spirit of Christ within us desires that we become like Christ, He is the only One who can fill us with Christlikeness. We don't know where we are deficient, which things in our character are displeasing to the Lord, and how to overcome them. The glory of the Father, the Son and the Holy Spirit is nothing that can be imagined, worked toward, or understood. It has to be revealed; it has to be experienced personally. God's glory is too multi-faceted and too supernatural to approach with mere human understanding. Spiritual truths are revealed, not arrived at by reason. (Read 1 Corinthians 2:9-16; 2 Corinthians 3:17-18; Isaiah 55:8-9)

The Holy Spirit shows us who we are inside. Without the Holy Spirit, we do not know how or what to change in our character, let alone how to go about the process of transformation. I know some things about myself, and I certainly know myself better than anyone else knows me, but there are parts of me that I don't understand—and there are motives, values, and attitudes which are a mystery to me. Furthermore, I don't know everything there is to know about God and His character. I have bits and pieces which have been revealed to me both in His Word and by living in Him and with Him, but the longer I walk with Him the more I realize how little I understand. If I don't fully know myself and I don't fully know God, how can I fully change? That is where the Holy Spirit living within me comes in. He reveals my inner being and reveals God's nature to me, but only a little at a time. Too much at one time would be overwhelming.

Paul talked about the need for the Holy Spirit to do this work in Romans 7:14-25. "We know that the law is spiritual; but I am unspiritual, sold as a slave to sin. I do not understand what I do. For what I want to do I do not do, but what I hate I do. And if I do what I do not want to do, I agree that the law is good. As it is, it is no longer I myself who do it, but it is sin living in me. For I know that good itself does not dwell in me, that is, in my sinful nature. For I have the desire to do what is good, but I cannot carry it out. For I do not do the good I want to do, but the evil I do not want to do—this I keep on doing. Now if I do what I do not want to do, it is no longer I who do it, but it is sin living in me that does it. So I find this law at work: Although I want to do good, evil is right there with me. For in my inner being I delight in God's law; but I see another law at work in me, waging war against the law of my mind and making me a prisoner of the law of sin at work within me. What a wretched man I am! Who will rescue me from this body that is subject to death? Thanks be to God, who delivers me through Jesus Christ our Lord! So then, I myself in my mind am a slave to God's law, but in my sinful nature a slave to the law of sin."

There are times in my life when I will go through a time of not knowing what God's Spirit is doing. I know that He is leading me, but I can't figure out why I need to go through the trial I am suffering. Later on, however, I realize that God has been at work within me to change me. Only after the process is over do I realize how God has been at work and why He has been concentrating on that particular attitude or behavior.

For example, in the first church I pastored there was a terrible split in the church. I thought that I could bring healing to both factions, but I ended up having to resign. It was a very painful experience for both me and my wife. However, I realized after the dust had settled and we had time to reflect on what happened, that God had been working on me about depending only on Him in the midst of trials and that He had been using this trial to free me from depending on the opinions of people for my self-worth. I still have a long way to go in getting my self-worth only from God, but that particular trial was tailor-made for me at that period in my life. Only after the process was over did I realize how much God had been at work within me to change that particular attitude.

The agents and the process of transformation

The only agents of transformation are God's Word and God's Spirit. This has some deep implications for us as believers.

First, if we are not habitually and personally feeding upon God's Word, we will not be transformed. Those Christians who get their only exposure to the Bible at church on Sunday morning will not grow toward maturity. I'm not saying they're not bound for Heaven, but rather that their maturity will be blunted. Some will go back to their old habits and lifestyle which they had before they became believers; others will coast along and spiritually grow slowly or not at all.

Second, we have to be born of the Spirit in order to be transformed. Those who are trying to be good Christians without being born again will be frustrated trying to do the work of the Spirit through self-effort and conformity to outside standards. The result is either pride, despair, or cycles between those two extremes. Jesus said that we must be born again in order to be transformed into the image of Christ.

Third, God's Spirit will use God's Word for our transformation. Jesus said that the Spirit of truth will guide us into all truth, but it cannot guide us into that which we don't know. I find that when I need guidance from the Lord, He will bring a Scripture to mind—but it is a Scripture I have meditated on beforehand, memorized, or been taught. Those who are subject to being deceived and misled are those who have not personalized the Word of God or made it an important part of their lives. This is why Paul says both to the Ephesians and the Colossians that they were to speak to one another with psalms, hymns and spiritual songs and were to teach and admonish one another with all wisdom. The more we encourage one another with Scripture, the more that we grow in Christ. Paul also says "speaking the truth in love, we will grow to become in every respect the mature body of him who is the head, that is, Christ." (Ephesians 4:15) We are responsible for helping each other to grow spiritually. (Read also Ephesians 1:3; 2 Timothy 3:16-17; Ephesians 5:19)

Fourth, God's Word needs God's Spirit to bring us to the knowledge of the truth. There are 31,102 verses in the entire Bible. There is no way that we are going to know or keep all of those verses in mind, but God's Spirit will bring the right verses to mind at the right time. That's why Jesus said that the Holy Spirit would search all things—the deep things of God. Only the Spirit of God knows the thoughts of God. If we try to keep God's Word through our own natural understanding, we end up in legalism, inventing our own rules and trying to keep them in our own power. We need God to reveal what He wants us to concentrate on in our lives.

Fifth, we need the objective Word (truth) to be made real to our hearts in order for change to take place in our lives. We need both the positional and the experiential: Christ and Christ in us. Colossians 1:26-28 speaks of "the mystery that has been kept hidden for ages and generations, but is now disclosed to the Lord's people. To them God has chosen to make known among the Gentiles the glorious riches of this mystery, which is Christ in you, the hope of glory. He is the one we proclaim, admonishing and teaching everyone with all wisdom, so that we may present everyone fully mature in Christ."

How does God transform us?

Christ living in us brings transformation. Here are four ways God uses the two agents of transformation, His Word and the Holy Spirit, in our lives.

1. Other people

God uses other people as examples of Godly living to show us our faults, to encourage us in being transformed, to speak truth into our lives, to teach and admonish us, to build us in the faith, and to love each other. Spiritual maturity and inner transformation takes place only in a nurturing community, where the various parts of the body of Christ mutually edify one another in the atmosphere of grace.

God uses other people as examples of His character that we can imitate. Often it is easier to understand God's character with a visual representation, a living reality of what God looks like. When we see characteristics of God reflected in someone else, it attracts us. Since we are being transformed into the image of Christ as we mature in Him, others see that maturity and know instinctively that they are seeing part of who God is. For example, I have a good friend who is a patient husband and father. He puts a great deal of emphasis on building his family, including his children, grandchildren, and great-grandchildren. The result is a family that is close and loves to be together. I have also seen this family go through some very difficult

> When I am walking with Christ, His Holy Spirit disciplines me when I make mistakes.

times. The closeness has come through much pain as well. He has been a wonderful example to me of what a Godly family looks like and acts like. His care for his family is a reflection of God's care for His family and His people.

The experience of seeing spiritual transformation in Christian leaders causes others to witness how God's authority brings about spiritual maturity. If our spiritual leaders don't reflect Christ's glory and character, then we receive a false picture of who God is. That's why Paul lists character qualifications when he talks about the qualifications for eldership (1 Timothy 3:1-7). True servant leaders are those who take care of the congregation, feeding them the Word of God and blessing them. Paul spoke of his care for the Thessalonian believers when he wrote: "We were like young children among you. Just as a nursing mother cares for her children, so we cared for you. Because we loved you so much, we were delighted to share with you not only the gospel of God but our lives as well. Surely you remember, brothers and sisters, our toil and hardship; we worked night and day in order not to be a burden to anyone while we preached the gospel of God to you. You are witnesses, and so is God, of how holy, righteous and blameless we were among you who believed." (1 Thessalonians 2:7-10) Paul loved them dearly and sacrificed his life so that they could mature. He encouraging them, comforted them, and urged them to live lives worthy of God.

2. Life circumstances

Some of our life circumstances are the consequences of our own decisions, for good or for bad. If we are walking with the Lord, He uses even our own wrong decisions to show us how we ought to live. There will always be times when I make wrong decisions, have wrong attitudes, or choose wrong behavior. But when I am walking with Christ, His Holy Spirit disciplines me when I make mistakes. He shows me the way to get things right with the Lord. When I know that something is not right in my life, I pray about it and God shows me something I did, or a wrong attitude, or unforgiveness in my heart. That's when I do what is right by applying God's Word to my life. Through this action, my conviction grows that His

Word is right. I believe in Christ and in His Word more deeply. (Read Psalm 119:105; Jeremiah 17:9; Romans 3:10-12; Isaiah 55:10-11)

For example, years ago I was working at a Christian tape ministry. A friend of mine, whom I hadn't seen in a while, came into the ministry to borrow tapes and when I saw him I really sensed that God had something to say through me to this brother. I asked him how he was doing and his response was that he had drifted from the Lord, was now divorced, his business was declining and in general his life was a mess. I exhorted him to get his life right with the Lord, as the first step. We prayed together. About a year later I saw him and he told me that the encounter we had in the tape lending library was the event that turned his life around. God used even me to speak truth into his life.

2) Other circumstances come at us from the outside; we had nothing to do with causing them and have no control over whether they happen or not. It is in these times that we learn how to praise Him for the good things that happen and trust Him in the bad things that happen. We discover that God is in control of our lives. He will not bring anything into our lives to destroy us, but rather to build us into His image and bring glory to Him. We learn to change what we can change and accept the rest. Romans 8:26-30 says, "In the same way, the Spirit helps us in our weakness. We do not know what we ought to pray for, but the Spirit himself intercedes for us through wordless groans. And he who searches our hearts knows the mind of the Spirit, because the Spirit intercedes for God's people in accordance with the will of God. And we know that in all things God works for the good of those who love him, who have been called according to his purpose. For those God foreknew he also predestined to be conformed to the image of his Son, that he might be the firstborn among many brothers and sisters. And those he predestined, he also called; those he called, he also justified; those he justified, he also glorified."

For example, we have some Yezidi friends who lived near Mosul, Iraq. The father had come to Tucson where we live and we had met him here. When ISIS invaded and took over Mosul, our friend's wife, 7 of their 8 children, and many other family members had to run for their lives. They were not able to gather any of their belongings, and had no passports. They were among the many who went up Sinjar Mountain and eventually escaped through the back side of the mountain. Through many days of walking they made it into northern Iraq and then into Turkey. When we met them, they were living in a refugee camp near Diyarbakir, Turkey. After about a year and a half, the wife and 5 children came to Tucson to join their husband and father. They rest made it to southern Germany. God has done amazing things for this family and is now using them to help other families.

God is weaving the fabric of our lives to mold us into His image so that we can be used by Him to make a difference in other peoples' lives. We can trust that it is God who works in us to will and do His good purpose. This trust flows out of a deep, heartfelt conviction that God is good and that He wants only good for us—that He is our shepherd, that goodness and mercy will follow us all the days of our lives, that the Lord is great, that His goodness is abundant.

There are also circumstances that come from Satan for the purpose of bringing destruction into our lives. The devil wants to destroy us, and he brings people or events against us in an attempt to keep us from following the Lord. In these cases, we learn how to resist Satan and to take authority over him. We learn that there is an intense spiritual war going on in the heavenlies and that we have to take hold of the things of God and resist the things which Satan tries to use to destroy us. (Read John 10:10; Matthew 11:12; James 4: 7; 1 Peter 5:8-9)

For example, on April 18, 2007, there was a Bible study in the morning in a Bible distributing house in Malatya, Turkey. 5 young men came to the study and expressed interest in learning more about Christianity after the Bible study ended. They then attacked three workers and slit their throats. All three of the men died. Two were married with children and one was engaged to be married. Two were Turks, one was German. Another member of the Bible study came late to the study, and when he approached the distributing house and saw that things weren't right, he called the police, who caught all of the young men. This attack was clearly orchestrated by Satan. It was brutal and meant only for destruction. God has certainly brought much good out of these three deaths, but it was satanic in origin.

4) Finally, circumstances can happen as a result of our effort and planning. Part of our walking with the Lord is that we learn to be intentional in our lives, choosing to do what is right and rejecting what is wrong. The more we choose to do what is right, the more we grow in Christ and become mature. (Read Philippians 2:12-13; Psalms 34:12-14)

3. Suffering and spiritual poverty

God's ways and thoughts are way beyond our imagining, and He also uses suffering and brokenness in the process of transforming our lives into the image of Christ. In 2 Corinthians 4:8-12, Paul writes: "We are hard pressed on every side, but not crushed; perplexed, but not in despair; persecuted, but not abandoned; struck down, but not destroyed. We always carry around in our body the death of Jesus, so that the life of Jesus may also be revealed in our body. For we who are alive are always being given over to death for Jesus' sake, so that his life may also be revealed in our mortal body. So then, death is at work in us, but life is at work in you." 1 Peter 5:10 adds, "And the God of all grace, who called you to his eternal glory in Christ, after you have suffered a little while, will himself restore you and make you strong, firm and steadfast."

Our weakness is our strength. When we are dependent on God, we are strong. We are devoid of self-sufficiency and empowered with Christ-sufficiency. It is not us, but Christ in us. We can be joyful, therefore, because the very trials which could ruin us become the foundation for a work of the Holy Spirit to make us strong in Christ, mature and complete, not lacking anything. Oswald Chambers said, "The Sermon on the Mount produces despair in the heart of the natural

> God wants us to be very active in the process of our sanctification.

man, and that is the very thing Jesus means it to do, because immediately we reach the point of despair where we are willing to come to Jesus Christ as paupers and receive from Him ... The bedrock of Jesus Christ's Kingdom is poverty, not possession; not decisions for Jesus Christ, but a sense of absolute futility ... The knowledge of our own poverty brings us to the moral frontier where Jesus Christ works."[37]

Jesus want to transform not just our actions, but our motivation, attitudes, values, and worldview. The spiritually poor person is perceptive enough to admit his or her own inability to meet God's standards. The first step to becoming spiritually real is to become spiritually needy. If we see no need, we will seek no answer, no filling for the need. Jesus is not against our happiness; He just wants us to find our happiness and joy His way. God doesn't want a bunch of miserable people. He wants transformed people. He wants to change the source and nature of our happiness. Suffering, if allowed to do its work, will bring us to brokenness. We have to get to the place where we acknowledge that we are nothing and that Christ is everything. Oswald Chambers affirms, "I will give my life to martyrdom; I will dedicate my life to service—I will do anything. But do not humiliate me to the level of the most hell-deserving sinner and tell me that all I have to do is to accept the gift of salvation through Jesus Christ ... The greatest spiritual blessing we receive is when we come to the knowledge that we are destitute. Until we get there, our Lord is powerless. He can do nothing for us as long as we think we are sufficient in and of ourselves. We must enter into His kingdom through the door of destitution."[38]

According to Jesus, a righteous walk with God begins with acknowledging our spiritual poverty. (Read Luke 16:19-26) It is interesting that one of the few places where the word "character" is used is in the passage in Romans 5:3-5, which says, "Not only so, but we also glory in our sufferings, because we know that suffering produces perseverance; perseverance, character; and character, hope. And hope does not put us to shame, because God's love has been poured out into our hearts through the Holy Spirit, who has been given to us." James 1:2-4 adds: "Consider it pure joy, my brothers and sisters, whenever you face trials of many kinds, because you know that the testing of your faith produces perseverance. Let perseverance finish its work so that you may be mature and complete, not

---

37 Chambers, *The Sermon on the Mount*, p. 12.
38 *My Utmost*, Nov 28.

lacking anything." By persistent steadfastness, we grow to full maturity. This is an active steadfastness in, rather than a passive submission to, circumstances. What began as a tentative belief ends as a fixed, unchangeable constancy of life.

God is more concerned with our character than with our comfort. The greatest good of the Christian life is not an absence of pain, but Christlikeness. For example, older people often have a maturity which has come about mainly through the difficulties in their lives.

I remember when I was a young Christian that I really believed that if I put the Lord first in my life that nothing bad would happen to me. I was wrong. Now, older and wiser, I have gone through many trials and tribulations and my understanding of scripture has deepened and come more in tune with the reality of life.

Suffering works the character of Christ into our lives. Remember, the word "character" in the Greek is *dokimyn*, the quality of provedness which faith possesses when it has stood up to testing, like the precious metal which is left when the base metals have been refined away. Metal has to be heated up and made into a liquid form in order to be poured into a different mold. Likewise, our character and faith are heated up in order that we might be poured into the image of the Lord.

4. Intentionality and effort

We are both active participants in the process of sanctification and passive recipients of sanctification. As Christians, we yield ourselves to God who is at work in us to will and do His good pleasure. We are dependent on the Holy Spirit in order to grow in our spiritual walk as God does that which by our own strength we could never do—put to death the sinful nature and walk in obedience to Christ. (Read Philippians 2:12-13; 1 Corinthians 6:11; 1 Thessalonians 5:23; Romans 6:13-15, 19; Romans 8:12-14)

At the same time, God wants us to be very active in the process of our sanctification. For those who think that there are now no commands for us who are living in the New Testament era, note that there are 1,050 commands in the New Testament and only 613 commands in the Old Testament. Romans 8:12-14 says, "Therefore, brothers and sisters, we have an obligation—but it is not to the flesh, to live according to it. For if you live according to the flesh, you will die; but if by the Spirit you put to death the misdeeds of the body, you will live. For those who are led by the Spirit of God are the children of God." Hebrews 12:14 adds: "Make every effort to live in peace with everyone and to be holy; without holiness no one will see the Lord." (Read also 2 Corinthians 7:1; 2 Peter 1:5-7; Hebrews 5:14; 1 Peter 1:16-16; 1 Thessalonians 4:3-4; 1 Corinthians 6:18; Hebrews 5:14)

Theologian Wayne Grudem says, "It is important that we continue to grow both in our passive trust in God to sanctify us and in our active striving for holiness and greater obedience in our lives. If we neglect active striving to obey God, we become passive, lazy Christians. If we neglect the passive role of trusting God and yielding to him, we become proud and overly confident in ourselves. In either case, our sanctification will be greatly deficient. We must maintain faith and diligence to obey at the same time."[39] We need to grow both in our ability to "let go and let God," and in our ability to pursue holiness and righteousness with all effort. As we do this, it is essential that we distinguish good works as a result of salvation and good works which lead to salvation. Nowhere in the Bible does it say that we are to earn our salvation. We are justified solely on the basis of grace through faith (Ephesians 2:8-10). The best terminology to signify our role in sanctification is that of cooperation. We cooperate with the Lord in becoming sanctified. God does His part by giving us the tools, the example, and the strength through His Holy Spirit to do what is right; but we have to pick up the tools, follow the example, and appropriate the strength to do what is right. Our emphasis is on walking with Christ, who leads us in the process of becoming like Him. We pursue Bible reading, prayer, worship, witnessing, Christian fellowship and the spiritual disciplines, and He leads us to do what is right and to avoid what is wrong. The focus is not on our effort, but on His enabling; not on doing, but on relationship; not on our work, but on His work in us. As we do this, God changes our motivation

---

39 Grudem, p. 755.

for sanctification. There are many reasons for doing what is right, such as the desire to be an upstanding person in the community or the goal of prospering through doing things for others; but only through walking with Christ can we do what is right out of love for God and for others.

The results of inner transformation

We have looked at how God uses the two agents of transformation through other people, life circumstances, suffering and spiritual poverty, and intentionality and effort. What do we look like when God's Word and God's Spirit transform us from the inside out?

We increasingly become more like Christ. As Romans 8:29 says, "For those God foreknew he also predestined to be conformed to the image of his Son, that he might be the firstborn among many brothers and sisters." This conformation to the image of Christ is manifested in six ways:

1. Our worldview is changed from a natural worldview to a biblical, Christian worldview. We approach life differently, learning and applying God's principles to our view of science, of family, and of culture, conforming to His thoughts and ways.

2. Our attitudes are changed. We have a different mindset about authority, work, money, and other people. God works in us to change our attitudes to reflect His. For example, we learn from God's Word that we are to love our wives as Christ loved the church and to be responsible for their spiritual welfare; we learn to be thankful to God for everything; we learn that we are to be generous toward the poor.

3. Our values are changed. Where we once valued leaving other people alone, we now value evangelism because we know that others' eternal destinies are dependent on what they believe about Christ. We value other people, realizing that all men are created in God's image and that we are called to love them. We value the life of the unborn, realizing that they also are created in God's image.

4. Our purpose in life is changed. Before we came to faith in Christ, we lived for ourselves and for our own pleasure. Now, we are gradually changed to live for Christ and delight to honor Him and do what He wants.

No one has to force us to do these things; we want to do them because we realize the more we seek to bring glory to Christ, the more we are fulfilled.

5. Our behaviors are changed. Where we once may have delighted in doing our own thing, we now want to read God's Word, seek the fellowship of other believers, serve other people, and seek to see others become what God has called them to be.

6. We find that living life in balance and full of the fruit of the Spirit— love, joy, peace, longsuffering, gentleness, goodness, faith, meekness and temperance—brings genuine satisfaction. We cease striving out of fear and guilt, and instead live with joy, motivated by love and gratitude.

We experience spiritual freedom. 2 Corinthians 3:17 says, "Now the Lord is the Spirit, and where the Spirit of the Lord is, there is freedom." Spiritual freedom is freedom from sin, from Satan's schemes, from the deception in the world, and liberation toward God and His ways. The Greek word used here is *elutheria*,[40] which means a life rescued from spiritual and moral wrongdoing; of a conscience no longer dominated by binding scruples (1 Corinthians 10:29); of a way of life no longer dominated by legal constraint (Galatians 2:4); and the liberation of nature from decay and corruption (Romans 8.21).

True freedom is freedom *in* Christ *because of* Christ. The Bible says that while sin brings bondage, true freedom is the ability to choose freely. The lie of the devil is that when we "do what we want," we are free. Jesus says that whoever sins is a slave to sin. When we think that we are free to make our own decisions, we are really in bondage to the devil, the world, and our own sinful nature. Our life as Christians is a process of replacing lies with truth.

Before I became a Christian I had a poor self image and a lack of confidence. I had believed the lie that I was not worth anything and I had allowed the world to beat me down. As I have matured in Christ I have replaced those negative thoughts with truth - that I am fearfully and wonderfully made, that I am a child of God, that I have been born again, that I am free in Christ to be whomever God called me to be, that

---

40 ἐλευθερία in the Greek.

I am dearly loved by the Lord, that I am not to compare myself to other people, that I have great worth in God's sight. Truth has set me free.

With every replacement comes relief, joy, integration, wholeness, and integrity—when the inside of who we are and the outside of who we are align in harmony. The world's system is based on the premise that man is not born in sin, that we do not have a sinful nature. The Humanist Manifesto II reads: "Ethics stems from human need and interest. To deny this distorts the whole basis of life. Human life has meaning because we create and develop our futures. Happiness and the creative realization of human needs and desire, individually and in shared enjoyment, are continuous themes of humanism. We strive for the good life, here and now.[41] Our lives do not have meaning because we create and develop our futures, but because God creates and develops our futures. The good life is not the here and now, but the life which Christ promises us in the world to come. The world is under an "illusion of freedom." Why? It doesn't see man as fallen and it doesn't see the cosmic struggle between God and Satan. It doesn't realize that we have been taken captive by Satan to do his will.

Much of the human potential movement, based on humanism, assumes that self-actualization is an end in itself, irrespective of its effects on others. It believes that the self knows best, apart from the traditional constraints of morality. All events, people, and things become instrumental in the actualization of self and become subservient to that goal. This belief ends with narcissism, the infatuation with self.

Character Profile
John - the Apostle of Love

John, the brother of James and son of Zebedee, was a fisherman on the Sea of Galilee, as were James, Peter and Andrew, and was one of the early group of apostles to join Jesus. John also wrote one of the Gospel accounts of Jesus, the three epistles called

---

41 *Humanist Manifesto II*, 17

1, 2, and 3 John, and the book of Revelation. One of the most memorable incidents concerning John took place at the Last Supper. John says in his gospel, "One of them, the disciple whom Jesus loved, was reclining next to him. Simon Peter motioned to this disciple and said, 'Ask him which one he means.' Leaning back against Jesus, he asked him, 'Lord, who is it?'" (John 13:23-25) John was totally comfortable with Jesus. He completely trusted and loved Jesus. It is no wonder that he is called the "apostle of love." His letters are full of admonitions to love.

We are to love one another as Christ loved us (1 John 4:11). We love because Christ first loved us (1 John 4:19). We are known as disciples of Christ because we love one another (John 13:35). First Corinthians 13 gives us the characteristics of that love: "Love is patient, love is kind. It does not envy, it does not boast, it is not proud. It does not dishonor others, it is not self-seeking, it is not easily angered, it keeps no record of wrongs. Love does not delight in evil but rejoices with the truth. It always protects, always trusts, always hopes, always perseveres." (1 Corinthians 13:4-7) Love is the moral foundation of everything we do in our Christian life. Love is what binds all of the other character qualities together (Colossians 3:14). It is the hinge on which every character quality swings. Love is the end of the law. Let's make love our aim.

The Westminster Catechism says man's chief end is to glorify God, and to enjoy him forever. If we make something for one purpose, it is not freedom to use it for some other purpose. If a shovel is made for digging dirt, there is nothing to prevent us from using it to pound stakes, cut a pork chop, or use as a saw. But the purpose of the shovel will not be achieved and any amount of striving to make our shovel into a saw will make it less productive and will be harmful to the shovel. It is not freedom for man to do anything but bring glory to God and enjoy him forever.

> We were designed by God to imitate Him.

We enjoy the ability to do what's right. Christ breaks the bondage of sin, making us free to choose to sin or to obey. We might sin, but we don't have to sin any longer. We have a power within us greater than the power of the sin. Romans 7:4-6 says, "So, my brothers and sisters, you also died to the law through the body of Christ, that you might belong to another, to him who was raised from the dead, in order that we might bear fruit for God. For when we were in the realm of the flesh, the sinful passions aroused by the law were at work in us, so that we bore fruit for death. But now, by dying to what once bound us, we have been released from the law so that we serve in the new way of the Spirit." For example, we know that part of our sinful nature is fear. Perfect love drives out fear (1 John 4:18). The one who fears is not yet made perfect in love. When we respond with fear, it leads us to do things which we know are not right. If we have had a very nasty divorce it can lead to lots of fears about another marriage. So we avoid anyone who might want to be with us and avoid making any kind of commitment to someone of the opposite sex. But we are very lonely. When Christ works in our lives, His Holy Spirit begins to deal with our fear, a little at a time. When we look at Christ's life, we see that He heard from the Father and did what the Father told Him to do. It is easy to let ourselves go and do whatever we feel like doing. It is easy to pamper our emotions and make decisions based on whether it feels good or not. But it is difficult to live a life of self-discipline and go against the grain of our own sinful nature and live a higher standard of righteousness than those around us.

Counselor and author Dr. Larry Crabb relates an incident in his counseling. A man opened a counseling session with an urgent request: "I want to feel better quick." Crabb paused for a moment. "I suggest you get a case of your favorite alcoholic beverage," he said, "find some cooperative woman, and go to the Bahamas for a month." The man stared at Crabb. He then asked, "Are you a Christian? Your advice doesn't sound very biblical." Crabb responded, "It's the best I can do given your request. If you really want to feel good right away and get rid of any unpleasant emotion, then I don't recommend following Christ. Drunkenness, immoral pleasures, and vacations will work far better. Not for long, of course, but in the short run they'll give you what you want."[42]

When we make our own well-being the purpose of our lives, we end up losing even the well-being which we sought. When we seek the Lord first, He brings us well-being, peace, joy, love, and fulfillment (Matthew 6:33).

We are enabled to truly impact those around us. We take Christ's glory into our culture. Christian character is very attractive to those who don't have Christ, since all mankind is looking for genuine morality and character. We were designed by God to imitate Him. When we act the way Jesus taught us to act, we are genuinely attractive to those who are seeking something to hope in. I am convinced that people the world over truly want to see the real thing—and are just waiting for someone to show them clearly what it means to live the genuine Christian life.

Vital conclusions

1. Our central purpose in life as a Christian is to walk with Christ. We do that through two major goals—learning and applying God's Word and walking by God's Spirit. In your life with Christ, you will either be building spiritually or be led astray by your sinful nature, Satan, and this world's system. There is no middle ground. You will not be transformed unless you put Christ first in your life. You put Christ first in your life by seeking Him above all else. When that happens, your life begins to gradually be changed into the image of Christ.

2. One of God's central purposes in your life is inner transformation. He is building a spiritual house in you so that you can be a place where God's Spirit dwells. You can either choose life or death, walking with Christ or living as a product of this world. God wants to set you free. He wants to bless your life and bring you into a closer relationship with Him. Allow Him to remold you into His own image. He promises that the new life with which you will live is the most satisfying life possible.

3. God has given you all the tools you need in order to grow spiritually and to mature in Him. He wants to make your life a blessing to you and to others.

---

42 Crabb, *Inside Out*, p. 77.

∾

We have discussed the agents of transformation, God's Word and God's Spirit. We looked at the process of transformation, talking about the role of other peoples' ministry and examples and the role of authority in spiritual transformation. We also talked about life's circumstances as change agents. We looked at the role of suffering and spiritual brokenness in bringing us to maturity. We cannot and will not mature without experiencing spiritual poverty. God is not interested in our comfort, but rather in our character. Lastly, we looked at the results of inner transformation: true spiritual freedom and freedom from the bondage of sin. We talked about true freedom being the ability to do what is right. We then talked about how our own inner transformation enables us to truly impact those around us.

Next, we will look at some theological issues which impact the subject of inner transformation. How we live our life depends on our understanding of God (i.e. theology).

EXERCISES, QUESTIONS

1. How are you intentionally seeking to grow in your knowledge and application of God's Word in your life?

2. How are you intentionally allowing God's Spirit to transform your life?

3. What are the most memorable ways in which you have seen God's Spirit at work in your life?

4. Who have been some of the other people who have impacted your spiritual journey? What was it about them which impacted your life?

5. How has God used suffering in your life to conform you to the image of Christ? Give a specific instance in which He did something which impacted your spiritual journey.

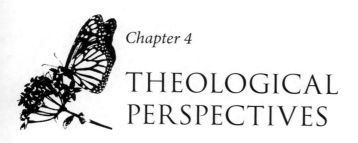

Chapter 4

THEOLOGICAL
PERSPECTIVES

The first church I regularly attended after starting my relationship with Jesus Christ was a growing charismatic church in Tucson, Arizona. God did amazing things among us, and I served as an assistant pastor there for about a year. The church grew quickly and everything changed constantly. Many ministries launched from that congregation, and many who were part of that movement are still serving the Lord today.

After being there for about six years, though, I noticed an ongoing pattern of teaching that said if we give our hearts to Christ and become filled with the Spirit, we would live a victorious Christian life. The teaching assured us of a victorious life, yet I kept seeing people who were dedicated to God and filled with the Spirit struggling with issues in their lives. I knew something more was needed. I began to question the theology behind the issue of sanctification—and I chose to go to Gordon-Conwell seminary outside of Boston to learn more and become better grounded in God's Word. There I reexamined all of my theology.

In this chapter, I want to challenge you to do the same thing. Even though you might not believe you even have a theological perspective, you do. Theology is simply the study of God. We will look at different streams of theology which may affect your view of sanctification, Christian character, and spiritual maturity. I understand that theological discussions don't interest everyone. I compare the study of theological issues to a mechanic who knows how to rebuild an engine. If he were to describe it to me, he would lose me in the first two minutes. I'm glad that he knows how to rebuild my engine, but I don't want him to describe the details. I just want him to do it right. However, in the area of theology, we have a greater stake in the issue. We do need to know more about theological issues because if we don't understand why we believe what we believe, we will be subject to error and unable to defend our viewpoint.

In the end, Christians will differ on some theological issues, but we are united by our love for Christ and know that our unity is born out of both our tolerance of and our ability to bear with one another in love. We love others because we have experienced Christ's love for us and His Spirit is working in us to transform us into His image. On our feet, we might differ on minor theological points, but on our knees, we are in agreement.

Part of growing in Christ involves understanding that our views are biblical views and our need to move our worldview closer to a biblical one. It is important that our theology is determined by Scripture, not by our upbringing, schooling, media, opinion polls, or our emotional state.

> Part of growing in Christ involves moving our worldview closer to a biblical one.

In this chapter we will begin with a deeper look at the theological terms of justification, sanctification, and glorification. Then we will look at the differences between justification and sanctification. We will look at some theological concepts which impact Christian character—eternal security and Lordship salvation. We will then discuss five views of sanctification and how these views impact our understanding of Christian character. Lastly, we will discuss briefly the role of the spiritual disciplines in sanctification.

Justification

American-Dutch Reformed theologian Louis Berkhof says that justification "is a judicial act of God, in which He declares, on the basis of the righteousness of Jesus Christ, that all the claims of the law are satisfied with respect to the sinner."[1] Berkhof lists some aspects of our justification by faith:

- It is not earned, but is conferred by God on the sinner who trusts Christ for his justification.
- It does not change his inner life, only his state, or legal standing before God. The sinner is restored to divine favor, not because of what the sinner has done, but because of what Christ has done.[2]

Romans 3:22-24 says, "This righteousness is given through faith in Jesus Christ to all who believe. There is no difference between Jew and Gentile, for all have sinned and fall short of the glory of God, and all are justified freely by his grace through the redemption that came by Christ Jesus." "Justified" in this passage is from the Greek word *dikaiow*.[3] In the active voice, it means "vindicate, treat as just;" in the passive voice, it means "be acquitted, be pronounced and treated as righteous." To be justified means to receive the divine gift of *dikaiosuny*.[4] (that is, righteousness).[5] The question that Paul is addressing in Romans 3 is this: "How can a man be just before God?" Sin has a curse associated with it. Sin carries death. Yet we have been set free from sin and death because of what Christ did. He who knew no sin was made sin for us.

Sin is not primarily a person's evil deeds or inclinations, but a person's striving for his own righteousness and justification. Hence, only the person who has died to sin, and is therefore justified, can do God's will. We can be justified only by faith in Christ, by trusting utterly and only in God's grace, which by definition is a free gift.

The essence of justification through Jesus Christ is this:

1. My attempts at self-justification are futile (Galatians 2:16).
2. I acknowledge my sin (Romans 10:8-10).

---

1 Berkhof, p. 513.
2 Paraphrased from Berkhof, p. 513.
3 δικαιόω in the Greek.
4 δικαιοσύνη in the Greek.
5 BibleWorks 9.0 (Friberg Lexicon) on δικαιόω.

3. When I acknowledge my sin, Christ forgives me of my sin and cleanses me from all unrighteousness (Colossians 2:13-14).

4. I stand righteous before God because Christ substituted His righteousness for my sin. I am justified, redeemed, and I have a new nature implanted in me which gives me the power not to sin (2 Corinthians 5:21).

This pattern of repentance and Christ's forgiveness leading to redemption and a new nature repeats itself throughout our Christian life. With each area that God reveals to us, we need to realize our own sinfulness and then receive the forgiveness that Christ brings to us.

Character Profile
Elijah - Conviction

Elijah was a prophet during the reign of the evil King Ahab, a time when there was great apostasy from the Lord. Elijah had prophesied that there would be no rain for three years and therefore famine in Samaria, and Ahab blamed the famine on Elijah, not on his own actions. Elijah challenged the prophets of Baal to a showdown on Mt. Carmel. He challenged them to make an altar, cut a bull, and put it on the altar, and then entreat Baal to send down fire from Heaven to burn up the sacrifice. He would then do the same—but call on the name of the Lord. When the prophets of Baal called on their god from morning until noon, nothing happened. They cut themselves and cried out to Baal, but still he didn't respond. Elijah mocked them. "Shout louder!" he said. "Surely he is a god! Perhaps he is deep in thought, or busy, or traveling. Maybe he is sleeping and must be awakened." (1 Kings 18:27) Elijah rebuilt the altar of the Lord, dug a trench around it, and put water on the bull three times. Then he prayed, "Lord, the God of Abraham, Isaac and Israel, let it be known today that you are God in Israel and that I am your servant and have done all these things at your command. Answer me, Lord, answer me, so these people will know that you, Lord, are God, and that you are turning their hearts back again." (1 Kings 18:36-37) Fire came down from Heaven and consumed not just the offering, but the water in the trenches. When the people saw it they fell on the faces, repented, and cried out, "The Lord—he is God! The Lord—he is God!" (1 Kings 18:39)

As believers, we are to be gentle as a lamb but as bold as a lion. Elijah demonstrated the lion side of God. Jesus was both the suffering servant (read Isaiah 53) and the coming King who arrives on a white horse (Revelation 19:11). When He comes again, "coming out of his mouth is a sharp sword with which to strike down the nations. 'He will rule them with an iron scepter.' He treads the winepress of the fury of the wrath of God Almighty." (Revelation 19:15) Jesus embodied gentleness, humility and meekness as well as boldness, courage and conviction. We are called to stand up against the injustices of this world and challenge the ungodliness of our culture. For example, John Wilberforce, a Parliamentarian, stood up against the slavery trade in the British Empire and it was abolished. What is the cause for which you are willing to risk everything to stand against injustice and ungodliness?

Sanctification

Inner transformation is referred to in theological terms as sanctification. When we are justified through what Christ has done on the cross and His Spirit lives within us, that same Spirit begins the process of making us holy through the process of sanctification. Author and theologian Millard Erickson defines sanctification as "the continued transformation of moral and spiritual character so that the believer's life actually comes to mirror the standing he or she already has in God's sight."[6] Berkhof adds that sanctification is "that gracious and continuous operation of the Holy Spirit, by which He delivers the justified sinner from the pollution of sin, renews his whole nature in the image of God, and enables him to

---

6 *Christian Theology*, Millard J. Erickson, Baker Books, Grand Rapids, Michigan, 1983, p. 890.

perform good works."[7] Berkhof says sanctification consists fundamentally and primarily in a divine operation in the soul, whereby the holy disposition born in regeneration is strengthened and its holy exercises are increased."[8] It is a work of God, but man cooperates in the process. First Thessalonians 5:23 says, "May God himself, the God of peace, sanctify you through and through. May your whole spirit, soul and body be kept blameless at the coming of our Lord Jesus Christ." Hebrews 13:20-21 adds, "May the God of peace, who through the blood of the eternal covenant brought back from the dead our Lord Jesus, that great Shepherd of the sheep, equip you with everything good for doing his will, and may he work in us what is pleasing to him, through Jesus Christ, to whom be glory forever and ever." Sanctification is a fruit of our union of life with Jesus Christ, and its manifestation in Christian virtues is the work of the Spirit.

Berkhof continues, saying that sanctification consists of two parts: a) the mortification of the old man, "that act of God whereby the pollution and corruption of human nature that results from sin is gradually removed," and b) the quickening of the new man, "that act of God whereby the holy disposition of the soul is strengthened, holy exercises are increased, and thus a new course of life engendered and promoted."[9] The two processes of mortification of the old self and quickening of the new self happen gradually, but also simultaneously. The old man is put to death and the new man is strengthened.

Romans 6:4-11 reads: "We were therefore buried with him through baptism into death in order that, just as Christ was raised from the dead through the glory of the Father, we too may live a new life. For if we have been united with him in a death like his, we will certainly also be united with him in a resurrection like his. For we know that our old self was crucified with him so that the body ruled by sin might be done away with, that we should no longer be slaves to sin—because anyone

7 *Systematic Theology*, L. Berkhof, Wm. B. Eerdmans Publishing Co, Grand Rapids, MI, 1941, p. 532.
8 Ibid, p. 532.
9 Ibid, p. 533.

who has died has been set free from sin. Now if we died with Christ, we believe that we will also live with him. For we know that since Christ was raised from the dead, he cannot die again; death no longer has mastery over him. The death he died, he died to sin once for all; but the life he lives, he lives to God. In the same way, count yourselves dead to sin but alive to God in Christ Jesus."

Sanctification also affects the whole man: body and soul, intellect, affections, and will. The doctrine known as "total depravity" says that every part of our being was blemished by the taint of sin. Sanctification, then, is the renewal of every part of our being into the image of Christ. The body is the organ or instrument of the sinful soul, through which the sinful inclinations and habits and passions express themselves.[10]

Sanctification affects the following four faculties of the soul:

1. **The understanding.** I don't know what I don't know. I am unaware of how depraved I am until God's Spirit reveals to me the depth of distortion in my thinking. When I am remade into the image of Christ, my understanding comes to resemble Christ and His way of thinking. (Read Romans 12:1-2; Jeremiah 31:34; John 6:45)

2. **The will.** As I am sanctified, I begin to desire things which were not even part of my consciousness before. I desire purity. I want to learn about prayer. I desire to be with the same Christians that I tried to avoid previously. I spend my time memorizing Scripture which I used to think was solely a product of human thinking. (Read Ezekiel 36:25-27; Philippians 2:12-13)

3. **The passions.** Before I came to Christ, I was enslaved by all kinds of passions and pleasures. I was led by my sinful nature and desired to fulfill the desires which came from that nature. Now that I am a believer, I develop different, Godly passions for the Bible, for helping the poor, and for moral righteousness. (Read Romans 7:5-6; Titus 3:3-5; Galatians 5:24)

---

10 Ibid, p. 533.

4. **The conscience.** Before I became a believer, my conscience was seared, blunted, and corrupted. I knew deep down inside what was truly right and wrong, but I rationalized that what I was thinking and doing was right for me. There was a disconnect between what I knew instinctively and what I thought and did. (Read Titus 1:15; Hebrews 9:14; Hebrews 10:22)

God is the one who initiated the process of sanctification and who will carry it on until I am made perfect. He gives me both the desire to become like Him and the power to get there. Sanctification also takes place both in the subconscious and the conscious life. The Christian life of sanctification is partly a process of the unconscious becoming conscious. If I knew all the areas of sin in my life at once, I would be overwhelmed, so God illumines gradually those

> Sanctification is usually a lengthy process and never reaches perfection in this life.

areas of sin which are unconscious and brings them to my attention. We are quite content with ourselves until circumstances, God's Word, prayer, or other believers point out areas of sin in our lives. Finally, sanctification is usually a lengthy process and never reaches perfection in this life. Berkhof says that our sanctification becomes perfect upon death. Even Paul says that he has not arrived, but he is on the path. In Philippians 3:12-14, Paul says he was pressing on to win the prize, but he had not yet attained all that God had promised him. The key is not giving up as we walk the path.

Glorification

Glorification is the final step in the application of redemption. It will happen when Christ returns, raises from the dead all believers who have died and gives them a new, imperishable, glorious, powerful, and spiritual body (1 Corinthians 15:42-44). Then He will change the bodies of all believers who remain alive, thereby giving all believers perfect resurrection bodies like his own. Glorification is the salvation of both the believer and the creation, as we shall see. We are being prepared for an inheritance that is glorious. 1 Peter 1:3-5 says, "Praise be to the God and Father of our Lord

Jesus Christ! In his great mercy he has given us new birth into a living hope through the resurrection of Jesus Christ from the dead, and into an inheritance that can never perish, spoil or fade. This inheritance is kept in heaven for you, who through faith are shielded by God's power until the coming of the salvation that is ready to be revealed in the last time."

The bodies we inherit will be like Christ's resurrected body, yet will be recognizable as our earthly bodies. Our bodies will be changed, but not completely remade. These new bodies will be imperishable, powerful, and spiritual. As believers, we are being transformed in our souls while here on Earth, but will be transformed in our bodies at the second coming of Christ. The heavens and the Earth will be transformed as well. The Bible speaks of the yearning of nature for this transformation. The whole creation groans inwardly for the redemption of all things (Romans 8:22). There are also passages which talk about those who are not believers being raised in order to face the final judgment. (Read Acts 24:15; Matthew 25:31-46; Daniel 12:2)

The process of glorification began when we were justified by Christ's death on the cross, continues as we are sanctified and become like Him, and will be completed when Christ comes again. We will become perfect, morally and spiritually, as He is perfect. This glorification will include a full vindication for all the wrongs which have been done to us while on Earth, the removal of temptation and of our sinful nature, and a fullness of knowledge and wisdom. We will find ourselves in perfect bodies in a perfect environment with a perfect God forever. This future glorification aids the process of sanctification by giving us hope to endure our journey of life in the midst of suffering and discouragement. First Thessalonians 4:18 says that we are to encourage each other with the thought of the resurrection of our bodies. We also receive hope knowing that whatever wrongs we have endured here on Earth will be made right. God will judge those who have done wrong, but will reward those who are righteous. Finally, glorification is a reminder that our home is not here, but in Heaven. We are citizens of a different kingdom and as believers, we are called to become more like that kingdom and like the King who reigns in that kingdom.

The differences between justification and sanctification

In this section we will look at the differences between justification and sanctification. It is important to understand these differences, so I will expound on these differences in some detail. First, however, let's look at a chart summarizing the differences.

JUSTIFICATION	SANCTIFICATION
Removal of guilt	Removal of pollution
Legal standing	Internal condition
Once for all time	Continuous throughout life
New birth	Progressive growth
Entirely God's work	We cooperate
Perfect in this life	Not perfect in this life
Positional righteousness	Practical righteousness
The same in all Christians	Greater in some than in others
Christ's work for me	Christ's work in me
Benefit: eternal life	Benefit: eternal rewards
Inclusive invitation	Exclusive invitation

Removal of guilt / removal of pollution: Justification removes the guilt of sin and restores the sinner to all the rights inherent in his state as a child of God, including an eternal inheritance. Sanctification removes the pollution of sin and renews the sinner ever-increasingly in conformity with the image of God.[11] When we come to Christ and ask for forgiveness for our sins, we are declared not guilty. Our sins are forgiven and we have a legal standing of righteousness before God. But that doesn't mean that our sinful nature has been deactivated; only that we now have power not to sin and can therefore choose not to sin. God's Spirit will then begin to reveal to us the pollution (ungodly thoughts, unforgiveness, wrong attitudes, unbiblical motivations) which exist in our own hearts and lives.

For example, we work with refugees coming into American from the

---

11 Berkhof, p. 513.

Middle East. Once they immigrate to the United States, they have certain legal rights and can start the process of becoming an American citizen. However, their worldview, attitudes, values, ideals, thoughts, speech, dress, and behavior are a mixture of their native country and an American worldview, etc. The longer they live in the United States, the more they act and think like an American. Usually by the second or third generation, the worldview, values, attitudes, ideals, thoughts, speech, dress, and behavior of their children or grandchildren become thoroughly American. Likewise, justification is when you get your legal rights. You are a son or daughter of God. Legally, you have full rights as a child of God. Sanctification is when you become more like Jesus. Just like the immigrant who becomes more typically American, you gradually become more and more like Jesus, imitating his worldview, values, attitudes, ideals, thoughts, speech, dress, and behavior.

Legal standing / internal condition: When we are justified, we have a legal standing before God as one who is completely without sin. Sanctification is an internal condition where we become in actuality what we already are legally. Sanctification takes place over our whole lifetime. Our thoughts, will, emotions, and plans are in the process of being changed so that our inner self corresponds more completely with our legal status before God. Because we have been polluted by sin, we don't know the way out of our predicament. We neither have the knowledge of how to become right with God nor the power to effect that change. We don't like who we are, but we have no choice but to continue in the state we are in—unless God's Holy Spirit works in us to change us.

Once for all time / continuous through life: Justification is not repeated, neither is it a process; it is complete at once and for all time. A person is either fully justified or not justified at all. Sanctification is a continuous process, never completed in this life. Justification precedes and is the judicial basis for sanctification.

New birth / progressive growth: There are number of events that take place at the beginning of our spiritual journey: the gospel call (which God addresses to us), regeneration (by which God imparts new life to us), adoption (in which God makes us members of his family), and justification. Sanctification is a gradual, progressive growth toward Christlikeness over the course of our lives. We cannot be sanctified until we are born again. Sanctification is the outworking of our new nature. Those who grow up in a nominal Christian culture may have many of the same mannerisms, thoughts, values, and even worldview of those who have a legal standing of righteousness before God—but they have never been born again, are not redeemed, don't have a new nature, and are not sons of God. They have no personal relationship with Christ.

Entirely God's work / we cooperate: Once we are justified in God's eyes through what Christ has done, it is finished. Justification is God's work, not ours. Only Christ's work on the cross, forgiveness of sin, is involved. We are called, regenerated, justified, and adopted into God's family instantaneously. I believe that this legal standing cannot be reversed because it is not dependent on us, but on God. Sanctification, however, does involve good works. We are saved by grace, but saved to do good works. We cooperate with God, who is the sanctifier, in the process of sanctification.

Perfect in this life / not perfect in this life; Positional righteousness / practical righteousness: Because justification is instantaneous, we are declared perfect in God's eyes, just as if we had never sinned. This is our new legal standing. However, we still have a sinful nature, so we will always struggle to become in actuality what we have already attained. This is the difference between our positional righteousness obtained by Christ and our practical righteousness, when we become in everyday life what we already are positionally. Philippians 2:12-13 says it best. We work out our salvation with fear and trembling, for it is God who works in us to will and to act according to His good purpose. We do our part and God does His part.

The same in all Christians / greater in some than in others: Justification is the same for all Christians. All have sinned and fallen short of the glory of God—and all are saved, called, justified, regenerated, and adopted without any favoritism. Sanctification, however, is greater in some than in others. Some grow very little into the image of Christ; others continue to grow throughout their lives.

Christ's work for me / Christ's work in me: I am not active, except through trusting in Christ, for my justification. It is accomplished for me. Sanctification is accomplished by the working of God's Holy Spirit within me, changing me, and requires my active cooperation.

Benefit: eternal life / benefit: eternal rewards: The benefit of justification is eternal life. The only condition placed on the inheriting of eternal life is to believe in Christ. Salvation is by grace through faith; it is the gift of God. The benefit of sanctification is eternal rewards when we go to be with Jesus. We do not earn our way into Heaven, but rather we inherit eternal life as a result of what Christ has done on the cross. However, our rewards are dependent on our good works. God will reward us for that which we have done.

> The benefit of sanctification is eternal rewards when we go to be with Jesus.

Inclusive invitation / exclusive invitation: Salvation, justification is offered to all. Sanctification is only for those who have been justified, who have trusted in Christ.

Eternal security

Many of us have observed those who come forward in a church service and make a commitment of their lives to Christ, but do not continue to walk with the Lord—either immediately or after a time of walking with Him. The question in everyone's mind is whether that person is really a Christian. Is he or she going to Heaven? Are we Christians if we show little or no evidence of a Christian life?

The two classical views on eternal security are linked to two different strands of theology: Reformed Theology, also known as Calvinism, which teaches that those who are truly Christians will not fall away; and Arminianism, also known as Wesleyanism, which teaches that genuine Christians can fall away from the faith and are lost forever. Theologians have debated these two views for six centuries. A third view is more recent and called the Partaker Position, a term coined by author and theologian Joseph Dillow. This approach will be discussed in more detail after discussing both Reformed Theology and Arminianism. All three of these approaches are based on biblical evidence, but each interprets the passages differently.

1. Reformed Theology

In Reformed Theology, eternal security is referred to as the "perseverance of the saints." In this view, the saints—those whom God has regenerated and effectually called to a state of grace—can neither totally nor finally fall away from that state, but shall certainly persevere therein to the end and be eternally saved.[12] Grudem says the perseverance of the saints means that "all those who are truly born again will be kept by God's power and will persevere as Christians until the end of their lives, and that only those who persevere until the end have been truly born again."[13] He adds that those who finally fall away may give many external signs of conversion such as good works, but they were never truly born again. Grudem says there are passages which clearly state that God will keep and protect His own so that they arrive safely to the end of their salvation. For example, John 10:27-29 says, "My sheep listen to my voice; I know them, and they follow me. I give them eternal life, and they shall never perish; no one will snatch them out of my hand. My Father, who has given them to me, is greater than all; no one can snatch them out of my Father's hand."

If we are born again, how can we be "unborn" again, or undo the relationship with Christ? How can we inherit eternal life, which is life without time, and then in time lose that which is without time? American pastor Dennis Rokser says eternal security does not mean that all who profess Christ actually possess eternal salvation.[14] We can never know what is in a person's heart when they seemingly make a profession of faith to Christ. Grudem also asserts that those who continue in the faith show that they are genuine believers, while those who do not continue in the faith show that there was no genuine faith in their hearts in the first place.[15] He points to the example of the disciple Judas, whom

---

12 Berkhof, p. 545.
13 Grudem, p. 788.
14 Hixson, et al, p. 246.
15 Ibid., p. 793.

none of the other disciples suspected of being the one who would deny Christ. In the time of the New Testament church, there were also those who were false brothers and sisters (Read Galatians 2:4; 2 Corinthians 11:26; 2 Corinthians 11:15) who participated with the genuine believers in the life of the church, but without being converted themselves. Jesus also warned of those that do not remain in Him.

One of the most difficult passages for those who believe in eternal security is Hebrews 6:4-8, which says, "It is impossible for those who have once been enlightened, who have tasted the heavenly gift, who have shared in the Holy Spirit, who have tasted the goodness of the word of God and the powers of the coming age and who have fallen away, to be brought back to repentance. To their loss they are crucifying the Son of God all over again and subjecting him to public disgrace. Land that drinks in the rain often falling on it and that produces a crop useful to those for whom it is farmed receives the blessing of God. But land that produces thorns and thistles is worthless and is in danger of being cursed. In the end it will be burned."

Was this person who fell away a genuine believer, or someone who never made a true confession of faith? Grudem claims that the writer of the book of Hebrews is talking about those who were "affiliated closely with the fellowship of the church" and had "sorrow for sin" who "clearly understood the gospel" and had come to "appreciate the attractiveness of the Christian life…They had probably had answers to prayer and felt the power of the Holy Spirit in their lives, and had been exposed to true preaching."[16] They had a familiarity with the things of God, but had never received Christ into their hearts. They were dependent on temporary blessings and experiences, but had never decided to trust Christ for their own salvation.

2. Arminianism

Arminian theology (from Jacobus Arminius, 1560-1609), also known as Wesleyan theology (John Wesley, the great British reformer in the 1700s), teaches that there is Scripture that talks about the necessity of

---

16 Adapted from Grudem, p. 799.

striving toward holiness in the Christian faith (Read Luke 13:24; Colossians 1:29; 2 Timothy 2:5) and that warn against falling away from the faith (Read Ezekiel 7:20; 1 Corinthians 9:27; Hebrews 6:3). Arminians believe that we are saved through our response to God's grace (faith) and since our wills have a part in our salvation, we can also fall away from that grace. We have to will to be saved, and we can will not to be saved. God's grace can be resisted. There is no eternal security. Arminian theology also states that too much emphasis on grace will lead a believer to think they can act any way they want since nothing they can do will affect their eternal salvation. Finally, this position maintains that those who do not strive for holiness in their Christian life are denying the many commands about how to actively seek righteous living. This theology teaches that there is a human element to coming to faith—free will. Therefore, we can choose to follow Christ or not to follow Him.

3. Partaker Position

This third view of eternal security, proposed by Joseph Dillow, argues that those who have been born again will always give some evidence of growth in grace and spiritual interest and commitment.[17] A man who claims he is a Christian and yet never manifests any change at all has no reason to believe he is justified. The assurance of salvation, he adds, is found only by looking outward to Christ and not by looking inward to the evidences of regeneration in the life. Therefore, if a believer is looking biblically and dependently to Christ, a lifestyle of sin will be psychologically, spiritually, and biblically impossible. The Partaker view says it is possible for true Christians to fail to persevere in faith and, in remote cases, even to deny the faith altogether. For most, though, the danger is not loss of salvation, but severe divine discipline (physical death or worse) in the present time and loss of reward, and even rebuke, at the judgment seat of Christ. In addition, a life of good works is the obligatory outcome of justification, but it is not the inevitable outcome.

---

17 For a summary of Dillow's view of eternal security see pages 21 and 22 in *The Reign of the Servant Kings*. The whole book is Dillow's exposition of what he means by the Partaker position.

Those whom God has called into saving faith and regenerated by His Holy Spirit can never fall away from salvation, but rather shall be preserved in a state of salvation to the final hour and be eternally saved. This preservation is guaranteed regardless of the amount of works or lack thereof in the believer's life.

The impact on Christian character

How do these views impact Christian character? A major problem I have with Arminianism is that it leads to a Christian life of fear and condemnation. The emphasis is turned from God's faithfulness and ability to keep us from falling to our own motives, actions, and ability to somehow "hang on to God." If we are saved by grace freely, then we should respond in gratitude, not obligation. It is difficult to mature in our faith if we are motivated by fear of losing our salvation and condemnation of everything we do. The Reformed and Partaker positions assert that it is God's power, not human ability, that energizes and sustains individual faith. We are saved by faith, but faith comes from the Lord, not from our own willpower or good works.

If we do not believe in eternal security, then we are fusing together justification and sanctification. Yes, our wills are part of the process of sanctification and we will lose rewards in Heaven if we show no fruit of our salvation. But our position in Heaven (justification) is secure only because of what Christ has done. Eternal salvation is an either-or affair; you either have it or you do not. Fellowship with Christ is a process; knowing Him experientially is not all or nothing. There are degrees. Rokser says this: "Eternal security does not mean that since you know you are saved forever you now have a license to sin; rather it means that you have been given liberty to serve Christ with full assurance."[18] Romans 6:1-2 says, "What shall we say, then? Shall we go on sinning so that grace may increase? By no means! We are those who have died to sin; how can we live in it any longer?" Turning back toward sin is natural for those who do not have the seed of life in them, but for those who

---

18 Rokser, in *Freely by His Grace*, p. 247.

have the presence of Christ living within them it is totally unnatural to turn away from the life which dwells within us through God's Spirit. Despair and carelessness come when we depend on ourselves instead of the Lord to bring about sanctification in our lives.

What about the person who believes in Christ, makes a confession of faith, but doesn't continue on in the Christian life? Is that person a Christian? I believe that this person is indeed a Christian, since we cannot be justified, then *not* justified. Once we are citizens of a different kingdom, we remain citizens of that kingdom, even if we don't resemble the citizens of that kingdom. I had a family in my church who attended church perhaps once or twice a month, but other than occasional church attendance were not involved much at all. I wondered if they would ever catch fire and pursue their walk with the Lord. Then, one day they caught fire and began serving and pursuing a deep relationship with the Lord. They taught me that even when there are few outward evidences of faith, if the conversion is genuine, God is at work in their lives on the inside. Genuine Christians have the Holy Spirit at work in their lives and will eventually show the fruit of a changed life.

Lordship Salvation

Those who believe in Lordship Salvation say that the biblical call to faith presupposes that sinners must repent of their sin and yield to Christ's authority.[19] They believe that Jesus cannot be a person's Savior without also being that person's Lord. A believer must produce fruit that will attest to this genuineness of his faith. The gospel Jesus proclaimed was a call to discipleship, a call to follow Him in submissive obedience, not just a plea to make a decision or pray a prayer.[20]

The burden for those who believe in Lordship Salvation is for the carnal Christian, the one who makes a casual confession of faith in Christ but whose life has no fruit from that confession. Author John MacArthur, one of the major proponents of this view, says, "I don't believe that there is

---

19 Hixson in chapter 5 of *Freely by His Grace* in the chapter entitled *What About Lordship Salvation*, p. 97.
20 *The Gospel According to Jesus*, MacArthur, p. 21.

any such thing as a Christian with self on the throne. I think that there are only Christians with the Lord on the throne—some are obedient and some are disobedient."[21] MacArthur believes the old nature is eliminated when we become a Christian and are regenerated. Opposing Lordship Salvation theology are those who believe in a Free Grace theology. They contend that salvation is by the grace of God through faith alone in Christ alone and not by works of any kind, such as commitment or surrender. The Free Grace position holds that salvation cannot come by a combination of grace and human effort. If grace could be maintained by human effort, they say, then it ceases to be grace. Grace has no place for works before, during, or after salvation—either to obtain it or to keep it.[22]

> Salvation depends on God alone, not on any measure of our faith or commitment.

Although I believe that there are legitimate concerns raised by those who propose a Lordship Salvation theology, I side with the Free Grace position. Lordship Salvation proponents blur the lines between justification and sanctification. Certainly, we are called to become disciples of Christ and make Him Lord of our lives in sanctification, but justification is a free gift. MacArthur maintains that salvation embodies sanctification—that justification does not occur apart from sanctification.

In addition, I believe Christ's work is complete. Salvation depends on God alone, not on any human measure of our faith or commitment. Finally, being born again is an instantaneous event, an absolute transition from Hell to Heaven. It occurs through faith in Christ's work on the cross. We know the Lord more throughout our lives and that knowledge happens in degrees, with ups and downs.

The five views on sanctification

Stanley Gundry edited a book outlining five different views of sanctification with articles written by five different authors. All of these authors are biblically-founded evangelical Christians, so the opinions

---

21 Ibid.

22 Chapter 1, entitled "What is Free Grace Theology?" by Michael D. Halsey in *Freely by His Grace*, p. 7.

they express are not heretical, but merely different emphases about the process of sanctification. You likely received your theological training under one of these views.

1. The Wesleyan perspective

John Wesley taught the concept of entire sanctification, "a personal, definitive work of God's sanctifying grace by which the war within oneself might cease and the heart be fully released from rebellion into wholehearted love for God and others."[23] His view was that we could reach a point in this life where we have perfect love for God. This usually happens, he said, in a distinct crisis of faith—a period of doubt and internal conflict—subsequent to justification. When we are in this state, we have a genuine freedom from conscious sin and a turning of the whole person toward God in love to seek and to know His will, which becomes the soul's delight.[24] Through Christ and the indwelling Holy Spirit, the "bent to sinning" could be cleansed from the repentant, believing heart, and a "bent to loving obedience" could become the mainspring of one's life.[25] This perfection of love is the supreme end of Christianity—what we would call Christian character or spiritual maturity. Wesley defines the end point of sanctification as "love in action," a heart totally given over to God. Wesley's emphasis on entire sanctification has been modified and adapted by many in Methodism and in the Holiness Movement, which came out of the Wesleyan tradition. The emphasis moved from gradual sanctification that began after the moment of regeneration to a crisis of commitment on a single point of wholehearted commitment and devotion to Christ. This led to the adoption of "second blessing" theology or to the "baptism with the Holy Ghost" central to the Pentecostal experience.

2. The Reformed perspective

Minister and professor Anthony Andrew Hoekema defines sanctification as "that gracious operation of the Holy Spirit, involving our

---

23 *Five Views,* p. 17.
24 Ibid., p. 18.
25 Ibid, p. 19.

responsible participation, by which He delivers us as justified sinners from the pollution of sin, renews our entire nature according to the image of God, and enable us to live lives that are pleasing to Him."[26] This renewal in the image of God has two dimensions. First, it is God who sanctifies us and recreates us into the image of Christ. Second, we have a responsibility to seek to become more like Christ by following His example. Renewal in the image of God is not just an indicative, it is also an imperative.[27] Thus, sanctification is not something we do with our own efforts, but is a product of God's Holy Spirit working in our lives. However, we do not remain passive, but have a responsible part in applying the principles in Scripture to our lives. We are working out what God, in His grace, has worked in us. Sanctification is a supernatural work of God in which the believer is active. The more active we are in sanctification, the more certain we may be that the energizing power that enables us to be active is God's power.[28]

3. The Pentecostal perspective

Early Pentecostals, coming out of the Holiness Movement, talked of entire sanctification as a second definite work of grace, a crisis of experience called the "baptism in the Holy Spirit." This view has evolved into including progressive sanctification as part of the work of the Holy Spirit in sanctification. This baptism belief is still practiced today and is accompanied by the outward expression of speaking in tongues. The Pentecostal perspective, from the viewpoint of Stanley Horton who represents Assemblies of God theology, teaches some of the same view of sanctification as the Reformed theologians, distinguishing what they call instantaneous and progressive sanctification. They also believe that our dependence on the Holy Spirit for sanctification does not dissolve the believer's own responsibility.[29] They teach that we will never reach final perfection in this life. Entire sanctification does not take place until we are transformed at Christ's second coming.

---

26 Ibid., p. 61.
27 Ibid., p. 67.
28 Ibid., p. 72.
29 Ibid., p. 134.

4. The Keswick perspective

The term "Keswick" comes from a resort town in England where annual conventions "for the promotion of practical holiness" have been conducted since 1875. There is not a distinctive theology, but rather a tradition of speakers who represent a similar point of view. The emphasis of the conventions was on elevating the experience of our Christian life

> God enables us as we pursue the Lord diligently.

through the empowering of the Holy Spirit. They distinguish "normal" Christians (defined as the Christian life exemplified in Scripture) from "average" Christians who have lived a life of defeat in the Christian walk. They state that a life of "faith and victory, of peace and rest, are the rightful heritage of every child of God, and that he may step into it... not by long prayers and laborious effort, but by a deliberate and decisive act of faith...the normal experience of the child of God should be one of victory instead of constant defeat, one of liberty instead of grinding bondage, one of perfect peace instead of restless worry."[30] The road back to fullness in our Christian life is through surrender to doing the will of God, usually in a crisis experience of coming to the Lord in childlike trust and loving confidence on Him alone.

5. The Augustinian-Dispensational perspective

Those who hold to an Augustinian-Dispensational perspective on sanctification talk about the importance of defining the word "nature." John Walvoord defines the sin nature as "a complex of human attributes that demonstrate a desire and predisposition to sin. At the same time, in one who has experienced Christian salvation, there is a new nature, which may be defined as a complex of attributes having a predisposition and inclination to righteousness."[31]

---

30 Ibid., p. 154.
31 Gundry, p. 206.

Distinctives of the different views

One of the areas of disagreement among the different views of sanctification has to do with the amount of human effort involved in the process of sanctification. How much of a part do we as human beings have in doing what Scripture says to do—and how much is God at work within us both to will and to do His good pleasure? All views, it seems to me, include the necessity of both God's working and human initiative, so the differences are more of degree than exclusively one way or the other. For example, the Reformed view emphasizes the sovereignty of God in sanctifying us, while the Augustinian-Dispensationalist perspective focuses on the need for yielding our lives to the Lord in the process of sanctification. I believe in a balance of human responsibility and God's work in our lives. God enables us as we pursue the Lord diligently.

The different views have varying emphases on the need of crisis experiences in the process of sanctification. Two (Wesleyan and Pentecostal) or perhaps three (Keswick) of the views of sanctification emphasize the importance of some crisis experience subsequent to salvation. The Wesleyan tradition was balanced between the crisis experience and the ongoing work of sanctification in the life of the believer. Wesley talked about entire sanctification, but not necessarily as a crisis experience. In the Pentecostal movement, the "baptism in the Holy Spirit" is necessary, they say, for the "overflowing fullness of the Spirit, for a deepened reverence for God, for an intensified consecration to God and dedication to His work, and a more active love for Christ, for His Word, and for the lost."[32] The Keswick tradition talks often of "tarrying" for the Lord, waiting for God to supply us with power for victorious Christian living

Though I agree that it is necssary to have crisis experiences, times of confession and dedicating our lives to the Lord, I believe that the process of sanctification is better thought of as a life of dedication and obedience to the Lord empowered by Him. Too much emphasis on crisis

---

32 Ibid., p. 131.

experiences leads to an emphasis on emotionalism and a false belief in the power of a momentary decision, exclusive of everything else, to yield to the Lord. Sanctification is an ongoing process and perseverance is more important than times of emotional release and dedication.

A third area of disagreement is whether there are two natures (a sin nature and a divine nature) or one nature involved in sanctification. I maintain that nothing good comes from the sinful nature (Romans 7:18) and that it cannot participate in God's essential character or nature. There must be two distinct natures, with God's divine nature gradually ruling over the sinful human nature, which becomes weaker through the operation of God's nature upon it.

The last difference involves the extent of the victory which Christ has won for the believer. I see this tension throughout all the five different views on sanctification. Wesley and those out of the Keswick tradition emphasize the victorious Christian life. The Augustinian-Dispensational theology also focuses on the power of the new life in the sanctification of the regenerated believer. I have seen this difference threading through-out Christian teaching, some emphasizing the continued existence of our sinful nature and others the power of the regenerated life. Both views are different ways of looking at the same biblical texts. The difference comes from our interpretation of Romans 7. Does it describe the unregenerate man or the regenerate man struggling with his own sinful nature? I believe it describes the regenerate man's struggle, but I also feel we should not overemphasize the power of our sinful nature as against the power of God's Spirit to transform us from the inside out.

Character Profile
Barnabas - The Encourager

Barnabas was not a major person in the Bible, but we can learn much from his life. He was one of the early elders in the church in Antioch. His name meant "son of encouragement" (Acts 4:36).

The apostle Paul was dramatically converted while on his way to Damascus to round up Christians and bring them back to Jerusalem to stand trial. After he was converted, Paul went back to Jerusalem in order to join his new brothers and sisters in the Lord. They did not trust him, though, fearing that he was just faking his conversion so that he could find out what was going on in the inside of this new sect. Barnabas "took him and brought him to the apostles. He told them how Saul on his journey had seen the Lord and that the Lord had spoken to him, and how in Damascus he had preached fearlessly in the name of Jesus." (Act 9:27) Paul would've been rejected by those in Jerusalem had Barnabas not taken Paul under his wing, believed his testimony, and believed in him.

As believers, we are called to encourage each other, believe in each other, and stand by each other. First Thessalonians 5:11 says, "Therefore encourage one another and build each other up, just as in fact you are doing." We are called to be like the Holy Spirit, who is the encourager, and help each other grow in Christ. Barnabas came alongside Paul and helped him to be accepted among the believers in Jerusalem. In the same way, we are to be on each other's side, forgiving offenses, bearing with one other, and helping others to be what Christ has called them to be.

The role of spiritual disciplines in sanctification

Sanctification involves both human effort and God's enabling through His Spirit. In his book "Celebration of Discipline," Richard Foster talks about twelve spiritual disciplines divided into three groupings.

- The inward disciplines: meditation, prayer, fasting, and study.
- The outward disciplines: simplicity, solitude, submission, and service.
- The corporate disciplines: confession, worship, guidance, and celebration.

How do the spiritual disciplines differ from legalism? The spiritual disciplines focus on building the inner man, not on overcoming the old man. Legalism focuses on trying to defeat the old man through self-effort, but the spiritual disciplines emphasize moving closer to Christ so that He will enable us to defeat the old man and build up the new man. The goal of the spiritual disciplines is to tap into Christ's power to overcome by drawing close to Him, whereas the goal of legalism is to expend more effort to defeat the things in our lives which hinder us. The spiritual disciplines also enable us to exercise self-control. When I find, for example, that my mind is starting to wander away from the things of God and I am spending too much time thinking about earthly things, I know that a season of prayer and fasting will bring me back to a greater focus on Christ.

However, spiritual disciplines can become a form of legalism if our focus is on the method and not on our relationship with Christ. We can become so enamored with the disciplines that we forget why we are celebrating the disciplines. The spiritual disciplines can lead to pride and self-sufficiency instead of humility and Christ-dependence. Finally, we can put too much emphasis on some of the disciplines to the exclusion of the others. For example, we can be really good at the inward disciplines because we have a very quiet personality, but we neglect the outward disciplines. Instead of using the disciplines to take us out of ourselves and serve others, we become enamored with our own spirituality.

Vital conclusions

What difference does it make to our daily lives to examine these theological differences?

1. We have seen that it is easy to confuse the processes of justification and sanctification. This confusion can lead to a spiritual striving for what Christ has already done through dying for us on the cross. The result of this type of striving can be a life of anxiety and fear. We can also take our salvation for granted, which results in a loss of blessings in this life and a loss of rewards in Heaven.

2. All of our actions spring from our beliefs, even if we are unaware of the source of the actions. For example, if we believe that we have to speak in tongues in order to be saved (the Pentecostal perspective), we will struggle all of our lives to try to speak in tongues. We will consider ourselves second-class Christians, or not Christians at all, if we do not speak in tongues. What we believe has a profound impact on what we value, the attitudes we have, and how we act upon those beliefs. Ideas have consequences, and we as Christians have eternal ideas with eternal consequences.

3. To live a productive and fruitful life, we have to be grounded in biblical theology. Jesus says that no branch can bear fruit by itself; it must remain in the vine and can bear spiritual fruit only if it remains in Christ (John 15:4). If our theology is off, we will not bear fruit. This is the mistake of those who have a "liberal" theology. They try to divorce orthodox theology from ethics, believing that it is enough to do good works even though they don't believe in the orthodox faith. This eventually led to adopting ethics which stem more from the culture's social agenda than from a biblical ethical agenda. Many mainline Protestant churches today have adopted the sexual mores and social agenda of contemporary American culture (same-sex marriage, ordination of homosexual clergy, acceptance of abortion and macroevolution) rather than deducing their ethics from the teachings of the Bible.

∽

We have looked at the processes of justification, sanctification and glorification, and developed in more detail the differences between justification and sanctification. We have reviewed the three different views of eternal security—Reformed, Arminian, and Partaker—as well as the Lordship Salvation. We examined five views on sanctification and then talked about the distinctives of the different views. Lastly, we looked at the role of the spiritual disciplines in the process of sanctification.

In the next chapter, we're going to examine law and grace and their roles in the development of Christian character.

EXERCISES, QUESTIONS

1. What do you believe about eternal security? Do you believe that you can lose your salvation?

2. What is your theological past? Can you identify which of the five views of sanctification most closely resembles your own?

3. What is your own experience of the struggle between the old man and the new man, and between the downward pull of your sinful nature and the upward pull of God's Spirit dwelling within you?

4. What are your habits of building the spiritual man, or of sowing to the Spirit?

5. Which of the spiritual disciplines (inward disciples, outward disciplines, corporate disciplines) do you find difficult to adopt in your own life? Which seem to come easily to you? What can you do to practice the disciplines that are difficult to you?

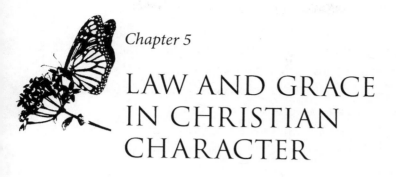

Chapter 5

LAW AND GRACE
IN CHRISTIAN
CHARACTER

S arah is what we call a "bad girl." A junior in high school, she could care less about school. She barely passes each class and gets mostly D's and F's. She has a very poor relationship with her parents and is surly and rude with her teachers. She spends her time partying and using hard drugs. She has even started selling cocaine, and she sometimes sells herself for sex in order to support her drug habit. She occasionally runs away from home with boys who promise her a good time. Sarah is full of hatred and bitterness.

Roger is what we call a "good boy," a nice kid. He is a straight-A student, a good basketball player, and has high ambitions of getting into a good college. He works hard and tries to obey all the rules, so much so that he goes beyond what is required by the school. He has very high standards for himself. Because of this, he is often critical of his school, his peers, and his coach because he feels they are too lax with the other students. Roger is self-absorbed and interested only in being the best at everything. His focus is on getting ahead, earning a high salary, marrying a good-looking girl, and being a success. He wants to be rich, honored, and successful in everything he does.

Galatians 5:1 reads, "It is for freedom that Christ has set us free. Stand firm, then, and do not let yourselves be burdened again by a yoke of slavery." Paul's words suggest that Sarah might be closer to the Kingdom of God than Roger. I say "might" because it all depends on the condition of her heart, how open she is to Christ. If she realizes that her life is a mess and truly recognizes that she can't overcome it on her own, then she will be open to the message that Christ died for her sins and will trade His righteousness for her sin. Christ is more interested in our heart condition than in what we have or have not done in our lives. Christ came to save sinners, not the righteous (Matthew 9:13).

The Pharisees were the Rogers of their day. They kept all the rules and even added other rules onto the ones which were listed in the Mosaic Law. They were meticulous and determined to be righteous. But they had no heart for God and no desire to help other people. They were righteous on the outside, but full of greed and self-indulgence on the inside. They were concerned with appearing righteous before others and loved the praise of men more than the praise of God. They were religious but had no relationship with God. They kept the minutiae of the law, but neglected justice, mercy, and faithfulness. They were Rogers—with no inward work of grace in their lives. (Read Matthew 5:20; Matthew 23:13-33)

Jesus died, not so that we can become like Roger, but so that we can be lost in the love of Christ and love toward others. We are not called to be good people; we are called to be redeemed people. Furthermore, the message of the Gospel is that we don't have to become a Roger to become a Christian. We don't have to clean up our lives in order to have a relationship with the Lord. No matter what we have done with our lives, we can ask Christ to forgive our sins and He will confer His righteousness on us. As Paul pointed out, the Galatians had fallen from grace because they let themselves be burdened again by a yoke of slavery. They started their Christian walk by hearing the words of Christ and believing on Him, but they turned back to believing they had to keep some or all of the requirements of the law in order to stand righteous before the Lord. Even though they

> We are not called to be good people; we are called to be redeemed people.

started down the road by faith, they veered off into legalism and rule keeping. As a result, they were not walking by the Spirit, but were being led by their own sinful nature. They did not realize that they had been crucified with Christ and were a new creation.

We don't have to try to be a good person like Roger. Our first obligation is to realize our sinfulness, even if we are more like Sarah. Our next responsibility is to believe that Christ paid the price so that we can be born again and have Christ's nature infused into our inner being. When we have Christ living by His Spirit within us, then we can become full of joy and love because we now have the power to become like Christ, made in His image. C. S. Lewis says, "If you have sound nerves and intelligence and health and popularity and a good upbringing, you are likely to be quite satisfied with your character as it is. 'Why drag God into it?' you may ask. A certain level of good conduct comes fairly easily to you ... You are quite likely to believe that all this niceness is your own doing: and you may easily not feel the need for any better kind of goodness. Often people who have all these natural kinds of goodness cannot be brought to recognize their need for Christ at all until, one day, the natural goodness lets them down and their self-sanctification is shattered."[1]

Christ didn't die to create a whole world of people who are content in their own righteousness. He died for sinners, not simply to produce better people, but to produce redeemed people, a new kind of people.

This issue of law and grace is a tension which runs throughout our Christian life. There are almost twice as many commands in the New Testament as in the Old Testament. Jesus came to us full of grace and truth. "The Word became flesh and made his dwelling among us. We have seen his glory, the glory of the one and only Son, who came from the Father, full of grace and truth." (John 1:14) Jesus was able to balance law with grace, to offer truth when truth was needed (such as His "woes" to the Pharisees in Matthew 23), but able to offer grace when it was needed (such as to the woman caught in adultery in John 8). He embraced both truth and grace equally and in full measure. It is difficult

---

1 Lewis, C.S., *Mere Christianity*. Chapter 10 entitled "Nice People or New Men." p. 112.

for us as believers to truly understand the balance of law and grace. We either tend toward grace—"then neither do I condemn you"—or truth —"go now and leave your life of sin." (John 8:11) Jesus both condemned sin and offered grace to those who have left their life of sin. He embodied both God's wrath and His kindness; God's condemnation for sin and God's forgiveness of sin.

Character Profile
Joseph - Forgiveness

When Joseph was seventeen years old, he was sold into slavery to some Midianite traders by his own brothers. The traders then sold him to Potiphar, the Egyptian captain of the Pharaoh's guard. After Joseph refused to go to bed with Potiphar's wife, he was thrown into prison and remained there until he was thirty years old. When he interpreted Pharaoh's dream by revealing there would be seven years of plenty in Egypt followed by seven years of famine, Pharaoh put Joseph in charge of the entire nation. When the famine in the region drove Joseph's brothers to Egypt to buy food, Joseph pretended that he did not know them and sent them back to Canaan to their father Jacob. When they again returned to Egypt, Joseph revealed who he was to them. The brothers were terrified that Joseph was going to take revenge on them, but instead he told them, "'Don't be afraid. Am I in the place of God? You intended to harm me, but God intended it for good to accomplish what is now being done, the saving of many lives. So then, don't be afraid. I will provide for you and your children.' And he reassured them and spoke kindly to them." (Genesis 50:19-21) Joseph's forgiveness was total.

Joseph realized two things. First, God is in control of our lives, even if it doesn't look like it. Joseph lost his childhood and youth because of the sins of others—his brothers, Potiphar's wife, and the chief cupbearer of Pharaoh. Nevertheless, he also realized that God was in control of his entire life and that He had prepared him and set him aside to preserve life. Second, Joseph understood that his walk with the Lord was dependent on his forgiveness of those who had mistreated him.

Five different views on law and grace

How we balance law and grace in our daily lives profoundly impacts how we live out our Christian faith. Most everyone agrees that Christians are not required to keep all of the Old Testament laws—but which laws are they to obey? Many Christians are selective in their application of Old Testament laws to their lives, and tend to single out the Ten Commandments as the principles to honor. But didn't Jesus come to fulfilled *all* of the Old Testament laws? Willem A. VanGemeren, professor of Old Testament and Semitic Languages at Trinity Evangelical Divinity School, says, "The issue of the observance and interpretation of the law has become more acute since 1955 ... Growing individualism and narcissism, the closing of the American mind, and ignorance of the Bible have resulted in an ethical crisis, affecting even evangelical Christianity."[2] The Greek word for autonomy is a compound of two words, *autos* (which means "self") and *nomos* (which means "law"). Americans today largely attempt to be autonomous and make up their own laws. Regarding Christians in America, evangelical Old Testament scholar Walter Kaiser Jr. says, "The current evangelical generation has been raised almost devoid of any teaching on the place and use of the law in the life of the believer. This has resulted in a full (or perhaps semi-antinomian) approach to life. Is it any wonder that the unbelieving society around us is so lawless, if those who should have been light and salt to that same society were themselves not always sure what it was that they should be doing?"[3]

Scholar and professor Robert H. Gundry lists five different views on

---

2 Gundry, p. 14.
3 Gundry, p. 75.

the relationship of the law and grace, or the relationship between Old Testament and New Testament ethics.[4]

1. The reformed perspective, discussed in an article written by Willem A. VanGemeren says that "God has spoken in every epoch of redemptive history, the Lord has loved people, and they have responded to his love by the triad of love for God (submission), law (obedience), and life (blessing)."[5] Order is maintained when people respond in these three ways. In the Garden of Eden this order was aborted and sin entered the human race. The reformed perspective asserts that the Old Testament law was not a means of salvation, nor was it a means of inheritance, but it was instead an instrument of sanctification. There is one standard of ethics which runs through both the Old and the New Testament—wholeness of life. VanGemeren says, "Ethical integrity is a wholeness of life. As we keep the moral law, pursue the perfection of righteousness in union with Jesus Christ, and walk by the power of the Spirit, we develop a wholeness that involves the integration of our heart, speech, acts and manners with the mind of Christ."[6] He also identifies three categories of Old Testament law: moral, ceremonial, and civil, and says that "ceremonial laws, civil laws, and the penal code have been abrogated, and the moral law has received further clarification in the person and teaching of Jesus Christ."[7] The moral law, he concludes, is summarized in the Ten Commandments.

2. The theonomic reformed approach is presented by American Calvinist apologist Greg Bahnsen.[8] He teaches that both the Old and the New Testaments are inspired by God and that the law itself taught that justification could not come through the law and good works. The whole Bible, including all the ceremonial and civil law, is perfect just like the

---

4   For this section I will be using the material presented in *Five Views on Law and Gospel,* edited by Stanley Gundry.

5   Gundry, p. 18.

6   Ibid., p. 58.

7   Ibid., p. 37.

8   Brahnsen's article on "The Theonomic Reformed Approach to Law and Gospel" is found in pages 93 through 143 in *Five Views on Law and Gospel.*

Lord Himself. The Mosaic Law, he says, is a covenant of grace, offering salvation on the basis of grace through faith, just like in the New Testament era. There is continuity through the Bible, he says, with Christ being the focus and aim of the Mosaic law or old covenant (Romans 10:4) just as he was of the Abrahamic covenant and promises of old.[9] He asserts that the old covenant law itself taught believers to die to legalism or self-merit, since the law, consistent with the Abrahamic promise, looked ahead to Christ and taught justification by faith.[10] Bahnsen also states that the Holy Spirit gives new power to obey God's commandments, and the Old Testament reached its finalized form in the New Testament coming of Christ with the new covenant surpassing the old in the realization of redemption. Finally, he says God's moral law "whether known through Mosaic (written) ordinances or by general (unwritten) revelation, carries a universal and 'natural' obligation that is appropriate to the Creator-creature relationship, apart from any question of redemption."[11] So then, Bahnsen says that the law of the Old Testament law "*itself* teaches us to die to legalism or self-merit, since the law, consistent with the Abrahamic promise, looked ahead to Christ and taught justification by faith."[12] Bahnsen says that "Since the Fall it has always been unlawful to use the law of God in hopes of establishing one's own personal merit and justification."[13] The New Testament, surpasses the Old Testament law in glory, power and finality, but there is no discontinuity between the two testaments. Both "are a reflection of God's immutable moral character and are absolute in the sense of being non-arbitrary, objective, universal, and established in advance of particular circumstances; thus they are applicable to general types of moral situations."[14] The law, then is good and the demands of God are universal. There is absolute continuity between the Old and the New Testament.

---

9 Ibid., p. 98.
10 Ibid., p. 99.
11 Ibid., p. 110.
12 Ibid., p. 99.
13 Ibid, p. 141.
14 Ibid, p. 142.

3. The law as God's gracious guidance for the promotion of holiness is presented by Walter Kaiser, professor of Old Testament Ethics at Gordon-Conwell Theological Seminary. He distinguishes between the weightier matters of the law, the moral law, and the lesser matters of the law, the ceremonial and civil law. The moral law, he says, is rooted in the character of God, requires faith, and is absolute. The ceremonial and civil law is illustrations, applications, and situationally-specific implementations of the permanent moral law. An obedient heart takes precedence over all forms of ritual. Kaiser also takes issue with the teaching that the law hypothetically offered eternal life to all who would obey it perfectly. He says that the law never could have brought eternal life. God's righteousness can never be attained by works in the New Testament era, nor could it ever have been attained through works in the Old Testament era. The object of faith was the same in the Old Testament as it is in the New Testament—the seed of Abraham, Jesus Christ.

4. The dispensational view is presented by theologian Wayne Strickland. There are three distinctives of dispensational theology: a) the literal interpretation of the Bible using a consistent grammatical-historical method of interpretation; b) the Bible's teaching that God's single program for history includes a distinct plan for Israel and a distinct plan for the church; and c) the glory of God in the purpose of history, worked out in "the program for redemption, the program for Israel, the punishment of the wicked, the plan for the angels, and the glory of God revealed through nature."[15] Foundational to the dispensational view is that there is an aspect of the law that has ceased in its validity and applicability.[16] God never intended the law to provide spiritual redemption for his people.[17] The Old Testament law contains no clear message of salvation or redemption[18] ... God is addressing his laws to a covenant, believing nation, giving no indication that salvation is

15 Ibid., p. 492.
16 Ibid., p. 278.
17 Ibid., p. 232.
18 Ibid., p. 233.

in view."[19] The Mosaic law was never intended as a means of salvation. The method of justification in the Mosaic era is identical to the current method: grace."[20] The Mosaic Law is antithetical to the Gospel and has no part in it. Law and grace as methods of justification must not be allowed to mix, or else grace has been lost.[21] Essentially, when Christ came, the usefulness of the law ceased. The authority of the law has been replaced by the authority of grace in the believer's life. Because the dispensation of the law is over and the law of Christ rules in our lives, there is no need for any lengthy, detailed, codified, external means of restraint as in the Mosaic law.[22] Strickland says that the law was given to the nation of Israel, who had already been saved. He also divides the purposes of the law into two aspects, the revelatory and the regulatory. The revelatory purpose is abiding, permanent, and reveals God's character even in the Church Age. The regulatory purpose, however, is temporary and, although binding for the Israelite, is not binding on the Christian church.

5. The modified Lutheran view, presented by New Testament scholar Douglas Moo, maintains that the law and grace are discontinuous. They are two successive eras in salvation history instead of being constant. The Mosaic law is basically confined to the old era that has its fulfillment in Christ. It is no longer, therefore, directly applicable to believers who live in the new era.[23] Moo also believes the law never could have conferred salvation. It was impossible and was not intended to bring salvation, but was for the purpose of leading the Israelites to Christ. The Mosaic law, by its nature, demands works. But since salvation can be achieved only by faith, the Mosaic law can have nothing to do with securing salvation.[24] Faith in the God of the promises, not obedience to the law, is seen to be the way to ultimate blessing.[25] The norm for New Testament believ-

---

19 Ibid., p. 234.
20 Ibid., p. 278.
21 Ibid., p. 279.
22 Ibid., p. 277.
23 Ibid., pp. 322, 323.
24 Ibid., p. 333.
25 Ibid., p. 335.

ers, Moo maintains, is the teaching of Jesus, and Moo says Jesus didn't expect the Mosaic law to continue permanently, but only until His coming. Therefore, the believer in Christ has been set free completely from the influence of the Old Testament law and is bound only to that which is clearly repeated within New Testament teaching.[26]

Character Profile
Boaz - Kindness

When Ruth and Naomi returned from Moab into Bethlehem following a famine, they had nothing—no land, no money, and no hope. Naomi said to the women in the town that they should call her Mara, which means bitter, because the Lord had afflicted her in taking her husband and sons (Ruth 1:20). She thought that all hope was gone. But Ruth began to glean in the fields of a man named Boaz, who was from Naomi's husband's clan. When Boaz saw Ruth gleaning and knew she was working hard to care for her mother-in-law, he told Ruth to stay in his fields and to take a drink whenever she wanted. He was kind to her, going out of his way to care for her needs. Boaz was a kinsman-redeemer for the land which belonged to Elimelech and bought the land and took Ruth as his wife. Both were acts of kindness to Ruth and Naomi. Boaz and Ruth were married and had a son named Obed who was the father of Jesse, the father of King David. Christ came from the lineage of David.

Ruth was kind to Naomi and Boaz was kind to Ruth. They were reflecting the character of God, who is kind to all. As believers, we are to clothe ourselves with kindness (Colossians 3:12) since we are called to imitate God in all that we do. That kindness is reflected in how we treat the poor, the oppressed, and those who cannot help themselves (as was the case with Naomi and Ruth). Leviticus 23:22 says, "When you reap the harvest of your land, do

26 Ibid., p. 376.

not reap to the very edges of your field or gather the gleanings of your harvest. Leave them for the poor and for the foreigner residing among you. I am the Lord your God." God made provision for the poor in the Old Testament, and we are to make provision for the poor and those who do not have the ability to provide for themselves. Let's be imitators of the kindness of God. Kindness flows out of God's grace.

The relationship between law and grace in Christian character:

It is important to determine how much of the Old Testament law we need to keep as New Testament believers. At issue is the contrast in Paul's writings, especially in Romans and Galatians, about the positive and negative views of the law. Equally vital is the relationship between the nation of Israel and the Christian church. Dispensationalists believe that the two are to remain distinct, while others believe the church becomes the extension of the nation of Israel. In addition, what is the believer's response to condemnation? The law brought condemnation with its rules and regulations on how to live a life of holiness. New Testament believers are dependent on grace. Paul addressed the letter of Galatians to the discussion of grace in the lives of believers. In Galatia, the Judaizers (a sect that believed Gentiles had to convert to Judaism in order to accept Jesus as Messiah) had fallen from grace because they were depending on the Old Testament law for their righteousness, insisting that believers were to keep selected portions of the Old Testament law. Finally, God's character is revealed through the Old Testament law, especially His holiness. Therefore, if we have an incorrect understanding of the law, we will have a distorted concept of God.

> How much of the Old Testament law do we need to keep as New Testament believers?

It is important that we be consistent in our use of the Old Testament law. What do we do with the ceremonial law which required the offering of sacrifices for sin? Are we, as New Testament believers, to keep the Sabbath? What about tithing? Should we try to impose Old Testament principles of civil law in our age, such as capital punishment for murder? The key is to be consistent and have a good theological rationale for the laws we choose to retain from the Old Testament and those we don't keep. In the New Testament, the Christians in Galatia struggled with the question of whether or not they were required to be circumcised. There are similar hot-button issues today, such as same-sex marriage, homosexuality, and the ordination of women. I have seen much inconsistency in the application of the Old Testament to present-day issues such as these.

Of the five views, I am most comfortable with the view presented by Walter Kaiser. The moral laws are affirmed in the New Testament and are binding on us as New Testament believers, but the ceremonial and civil laws were fulfilled in Christ. What is important is that we have a consistent and theologically biblical view of the relationship between law and grace and between the Old and New Testaments. Jesus summarized our relationship with Old Testament law in Matthew 5:17-20. He said, "Do not think that I have come to abolish the Law or the Prophets; I have not come to abolish them but to fulfill them. For truly I tell you, until heaven and earth disappear, not the smallest letter, not the least stroke of a pen, will by any means disappear from the Law until everything is accomplished. Therefore anyone who sets aside one of the least of these commands and teaches others accordingly will be called least in the kingdom of heaven, but whoever practices and teaches these commands will be called great in the kingdom of heaven. For I tell you that unless your righteousness surpasses that of the Pharisees and the teachers of the law, you will certainly not enter the kingdom of heaven."

Jesus fulfilled the law by bringing it to completion by His person, His teaching, and His work. The Old Testament law was looking forward to and anticipating Christ's coming. Jesus fulfilled the civil and ceremonial law, and confirmed the moral law. Jesus also states in Matthew 5 that

God's Word is still true. The law is as enduring as the universe—until Heaven and Earth disappear. The attitude of Jesus to the Old Testament was not one of destruction and of discontinuity, but rather of a constructive, organic continuity. Jesus disagreed with the Pharisees' interpretation of the law, but He never disagreed with their acceptance of its authority. He affirmed instead that the entire Old Testament was given by the authority of God.

Jesus also reaffirmed that we are to keep the commandments. The Pharisees realized that it was very difficult to keep all the commands, so they had relaxed some of the commands, and extended some of the permissions from the law. How did the Pharisees relax the law? They made the law's demands less demanding and the law's permissions more permissive. Christ introduced six examples with the terminology, "You have heard that it was said to the men of old … but I say to you." In these examples, the Pharisees had restricted the biblical prohibitions of murder and adultery to the act alone; Jesus extended them to include angry thoughts, insulting words, and lustful looks. They had restricted the command about swearing to certain oaths only (those involving the divine name) and the command about neighbor-love to certain people only (those of the same race and religion); Jesus said all promises must be kept and all people must be loved, even their enemies.

Finally, Jesus taught that effort and sincerity are not enough, and that our righteousness is to surpass that of the Pharisees and the teachers of the law. We are to keep the law by going to the heart of the matter—to the inner man, to a transformed heart which is obedient out of love for God.

Natural law and Christian character

Natural law is a quality in man that enables him to know God as Creator if not as Redeemer—or at least to know of His existence and in some respects what He is like. This rudimentary knowledge will then form the starting point for a fuller understanding of God.[27] For example, God is seen in the incredible complexity and beauty of the structure of the

27 *Baker's Dictionary of Theology*, article on Natural Theology by T. H. L. Parker.

molecule, in the beauty of nature, in the way that our bodies heal, or in the love of a man for a woman. God's eternal power and divinity have been clearly seen in nature. Paul says in Romans 1 that to miss God in nature means that we have deliberately turned away from God and have suppressed the truth by our own wickedness. Paul goes on to say, "For although they knew God, they neither glorified him as God nor gave thanks to him, but their thinking became futile and their foolish hearts were darkened. Although they claimed to be wise, they became fools." (Romans 1:21-22) In other words, God is not far from each of us, but some purposefully deny the obvious. Psalm 95:3-5 adds, "For the Lord is the great God, the great King above all gods. In his hand are the depths of the earth, and the mountain peaks belong to him. The sea is his, for he made it, and his hands formed the dry land."

God's divine power and nature are seen in human beings as well. We have a natural understanding of the existence of God and of what is good and bad. This is what we call our "conscience," defined in Webster's Dictionary as "the inner sense of what is right or wrong in one's conduct or motives, impelling one towards right action, and the complex of ethical and moral principles that controls or inhibits the actions or thoughts of an individual."[28] Some have blunted this consciousness and are no longer aware of it, but all possess an inherent, internal, God-given moral consciousness. Romans 2:13-15 reads, "For it is not those who hear the law who are righteous in God's sight, but it is those who obey the law who will be declared righteous. (Indeed, when Gentiles, who do not have the law, do by nature things required by the law, they are a law for themselves, even though they do not have the law. They show that the requirements of the law are written on their hearts, their consciences also bearing witness, and their thoughts sometimes accusing them and at other times even defending them.)"

All of God's creation is out of order and is yearning to be "liberated from its bondage to decay and brought into the freedom and glory of the children of God." (Romans 8:21) One day there will be a

---

28 *Webster's Dictionary*, article on "conscience."

new Heaven and new Earth and every redeemed person will inherit their glorified body and the whole creation will be renewed. Psalm 19:1-4 declares, "The heavens declare the glory of God; the skies proclaim the work of his hands. Day after day they pour forth speech; night after night they reveal knowledge. They have no speech, they use no words; no sound is heard from them. Yet their voice goes out into all the earth, their words to the ends of the world. In the heavens God has pitched a tent for the sun."

> We are filled with joy when we first believe in Christ because we are coming home.

∾

Vital conclusions

1. This chapter has concentrated on the relationship between law and grace in a Christian's life. We talked about five different views on law and grace—or the relationship between the Old and the New Testament—and what is still binding on Christ followers today. I have maintained throughout this book that character is universal, but that only Christians can actually pursue character transformation because we have the Holy Spirit's enabling power. God will judge all men on the basis of their character, whether they are Christian or not. Because we all possess an innate sense of right and wrong which is given by God, we will be judged based on that sense of right or wrong, even if we do not acknowledge God's existence.

2. When we are reconstructed into the image of Christ and transformed into His likeness, we are merely coming back to the original design which God had determined for us from the beginning of time. The reason that we are filled with joy when we take the first step of believing in Christ is that we are coming home. We are taking a step toward what we were made to become. God has also given us a conscience, an innate sense which agrees with both the existence of God and His absolute standards of right and wrong.

QUESTIONS, EXERCISES

1. Which view presented in this chapter most closely resembles what you have been taught?

2. Relate how you have seen others or yourself misuse Old Testament law.

3. Are there areas in your own life where you tend toward legalism?

4. Apply the balance between law and grace to the issue of same-sex marriage. If someone came to you and asked for your biblical stance on the topic, how would you respond?

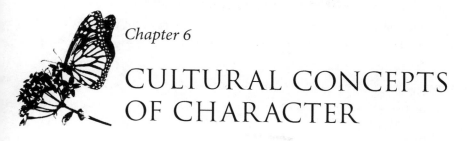

Chapter 6

CULTURAL CONCEPTS
OF CHARACTER

There is a cultural war going on in America, an ongoing clash of differing worldviews. This conflict has been characterized as the left vs. the right, liberal vs. conservative, secular humanism vs. Judeo-Christian values, unbelievers vs. believers, and Satan vs. God[1] This cultural war is gaining momentum and the divide between the two sides is becoming larger. The battle is more felt than understood because most people are not acutely aware of the cultural divide, yet it spills over into all walks of life—political, financial, educational, and religious. It separates people on ideological, generational, ethnic, and geographical fronts.

Even though I attended an Episcopal church through junior high school, I grew up a secularist. The schools I attended, especially the universities, were decidedly secular in their teaching and I was thoroughly liberal in my thinking. It was only after becoming a Christian at the age of twenty-six that my worldview slowly began to change toward a biblical worldview. It has been a long and difficult journey

---

1 Dennis Prager, in his book *Still the Best Hope, Why the World Needs American Values to Triumph*, divides this ideological war into three components: Leftist, Islam, and American. David Noebel in his book *Understanding the Times* divides the ideological conflict into biblical Christian, Marxist/Leninist, and Secular Humanist worldviews. I have chosen to limit the discussion to two categories, since I believe that two categories is the more biblical view. Culturally, however, they are right in including the categories they include.

transitioning from a secular humanism worldview to a biblical Christianity worldview. God's Holy Spirit continues to reveal to me thought patterns still in transition. It has been a struggle letting go of my old way of thinking and adopting a new worldview completely counter-cultural to the one that once dominated my thinking. When I began to engage in humanitarian and missionary work in Turkey, I discovered that the thought processes in every culture, and in every person on Earth, are also in transition. The struggle focuses on replacing thoughts that depend on human tradition and the principles of this world with God's revelation. This transition is unnatural for the person without the Spirit of God, but it is natural for those who have Jesus Christ as Lord (Colossians 2:8).

When Paul wrote in Romans 12 that we are not to conform to the pattern of this world but be transformed by the renewing of our minds, Isaiah 55:8-9 says, "'For my thoughts are not your thoughts, neither are your ways my ways,' declares the Lord. 'As the heavens are higher than the earth, so are my ways higher than your ways and my thoughts than your thoughts.'" God's perspective is not only different, it is superior because it originates from heavenly thinking, not earthly wisdom. Because we are in a spiritual battle with arguments and every pretension that sets itself up against the knowledge of God, we are to take every thought captive and allow God's Spirit to replace our thinking with His (2 Corinthians 10:5).

People believe lies about those who possess the truth.

I do not believe this cultural war is primarily political, although it is often manifested along political lines. It is actually a battle of worldview and values, biblical vs. non-biblical. The core issues are the questions of whether or not God exists, and whether the Bible is a God-inspired document. Those questions are key to determining the ethical standard on which to base our values. If there is no God, then we can believe anything we want and are free to come up with natural-istic explanations for everything in the universe. If there is no ethical standard, then we are free to do as we wish and do not have to be accountable to anyone. Former White House counsel and evangelical leader Charles Colson said that theologian, philosopher, and Presbyterian pastor Francis Schaeffer put his finger on the problem when he wrote that Christians in America see things in "bits and pieces" instead of "totals." What he meant was that many Christians don't understand how their faith intersects with life beyond their personal relationship with Christ. They know a little bit here and a little piece there, but what is missing is a comprehensive worldview and the ability to see day-by-day issues from a biblical perspective.[2] As Christians begin to apply a biblical worldview to daily life, it won't be popular. I have seen accusations against Christians increase over the past few decades. Where only a short time ago society had a positive perception of Christians, it now has a negative one. According to a recent World Magazine article,[3] military chaplains once had the freedom to talk about Christ with those under their care. Now they are restricted and face an increasingly hostile environment. Christianity is becoming more marginalized. In a United States Army Reserve training brief on hate groups in America, evangelical Christianity, Catholicism and "Christian Identity" are listed in the same context as Al Qaeda, the Ku Klux Klan, and the Nation of Islam. The military, along with nearly every other segment of American culture, is becoming secularized and hostile to Christianity. People believe lies about those who possess the truth. Those who are harmless as doves (Matthew 10:16) are characterized as wolves. When people turn away from God, they veer toward moral confusion and spiritual darkness, and acquire a blindness to discern true character. As Isaiah 5:20-23 says, "Woe to those who call evil good and good evil, who put darkness for light and light for darkness, who put bitter for sweet and sweet for bitter. Woe to those who are wise in their own eyes and clever in their own sight. Woe to those who are heroes at drinking wine and champions at mixing drinks, who acquit the guilty for a bribe, but deny justice to the innocent."

---

2 *Breakpoint* article by Charles Colson, Aug 30, 2000.
3 Pitts, Edward Lee, *World Magazine*, "Holding the Line," July 13, 2013, pp. 34-38.

The biblical perspective

A key passage that distinguishes Christian thinking from secular thinking is Colossians 2:6-10: "So then, just as you received Christ Jesus as Lord, continue to live your lives in him, rooted and built up in him, strengthened in the faith as you were taught, and overflowing with thankfulness. See to it that no one takes you captive through hollow and deceptive philosophy, which depends on human tradition and the elemental spiritual forces of this world rather than on Christ. For in Christ all the fullness of the Deity lives in bodily form, and in Christ you have been brought to fullness. He is the head over every power and authority." The term "takes you captive" in this passage speaks figuratively of carrying someone away from the truth into the slavery of error. The picture is that of a long procession of prisoners being led away with a rope around their necks. To understand the passage fully, it helps to learn more about the philosophy Paul was countering in Colossae. The Colossian heresy evidently encouraged the claim that the fullness of God could be appreciated only by mystical experiences for which strict self-denial was necessary. It was humanly motivated and executed. Paul challenged this heresy by stating that it was not necessary to have any mystical experience to add to what Christ has already done. Christ is the fullness of the deity in bodily form. The Colossian heresy also focused on syncretism, the view that all kinds of ideas flow together. Today, secular humanism aims to be syncretistic. It says there are many ways to God. It is necessary to have tolerance of the views of others.

The philosophy of the false teachers in Colossae was hollow, lacking substance or any foundation in truth. It sounds logical and helpful, but the roots don't go anywhere. The Greek word used is *kenys,*[4] which means "empty, without content." It is used of things which are futile, vain, and foolish. The basic problem with the tenets of secular humanism is there is no substance to its claims. It promises happiness, wisdom, and intellectual depth, but comes up lacking in all three categories. I am not suggesting that those who believe in the philosophy of secular humanism

---

4 κενῆς in the Greek.

set out to deceive others. There are very successful people who believe in its tenets, but any philosophy, thought, or religion that does not agree with the Bible is misleading, deceptive, and built on lies.

The source of this hollow and deceptive philosophy is "human tradition," in the Greek *paradosin*[5] which means "a handing down or over." In the New Testament, it signifies "teachings about ways of doing things that are handed down from generation to generation." We believe either what God has revealed or what people have invented. Human tradition is deceptive because it comes from the deceiver himself, Satan. Secular humanism is rooted in human tradition and begins with the premise that there is no God and therefore no divine revelation. One of the great passages in the Bible talking about humanity's descent into humanistic thinking is Romans 1:18-32. It reads:

"The wrath of God is being revealed from heaven against all the godlessness and wickedness of people, who suppress the truth by their wickedness, since what may be known about God is plain to them, because God has made it plain to them. For since the creation of the world God's invisible qualities—his eternal power and divine nature—have been clearly seen, being understood from what has been made, so that people are without excuse. For although they knew God, they neither glorified him as God nor gave thanks to him, but their thinking became futile and their foolish hearts were darkened. Although they claimed to be wise, they became fools and exchanged the glory of the immortal God for images made to look like a mortal human being and birds and animals and reptiles. Therefore God gave them over in the sinful desires of their hearts to sexual impurity for the degrading of their bodies with one another. They exchanged the truth about God for a lie, and worshiped and served created things rather than the Creator—who is forever praised. Amen. Because of this, God gave them over to shameful lusts. Even their women exchanged natural sexual relations for unnatural ones. In the same way the men also abandoned natural relations with women and were inflamed with lust for one another. Men committed shameful

---

5 Παράδοσιν in the Greek.

acts with other men, and received in themselves the due penalty for their error. Furthermore, just as they did not think it worthwhile to retain the knowledge of God, so God gave them over to a depraved mind, so that they do what ought not to be done. They have become filled with every kind of wickedness, evil, greed and depravity. They are full of envy, murder, strife, deceit and malice. They are gossips, slanderers, God-haters, insolent, arrogant and boastful; they invent ways of doing evil; they disobey their parents; they have no understanding, no fidelity, no love, no mercy. Although they know God's righteous decree that those who do such things deserve death, they not only continue to do these very things but also approve of those who practice them."

An understanding of God is natural and plain, and those who suppress that knowledge are without excuse. God's nature and power are so easily understood that a child can know God. His handiwork is seen everywhere and it takes a deliberate effort to turn away from the knowledge of Him. Those who turn away may think that they are wise, but are in actuality foolish and unthankful. For example, some humanists teach that it is perfectly acceptable to kill unborn babies, but morally reprehensible to kill whales. A lack of sexual purity is another clear indication that people are not walking with God. It's not unusual that where humanism is taught, the university campus, there is also much sexual immorality. Colossians 2:20-23 says, "Since you died with Christ to the elemental spiritual forces of this world, why, as though you still belonged to the world, do you submit to its rules: "Do not handle! Do not taste! Do not touch!" These rules, which have to do with things that are all destined to perish with use, are based on merely human commands and teachings. Such regulations indeed have an appearance of wisdom, with their self-imposed worship, their false humility and their harsh treatment of the body, but they lack any value in restraining sensual indulgence."

Secular humanism is not a religion or even a well-defined philosophy. It is a way of thinking.

Those who turn away from God are given over to the works of the sinful nature and are governed by that nature. The phrase "gave them over" from the Romans 1 passage is *parédoken*[6] in the Greek. It's God's judicial act of handing someone over to suffer the consequences of his wrongdoing. Those who are without God cannot reason themselves out of their predicament. Finally, those who have suppressed the knowledge of God will be held accountable for their decision.

Paul spoke to the members of the church at Corinth about human wisdom. "For Christ did not send me to baptize, but to preach the gospel—not with wisdom and eloquence, lest the cross of Christ be emptied of its power. For the message of the cross is foolishness to those who are perishing, but to us who are being saved it is the power of God. For it is written: 'I will destroy the wisdom of the wise; the intelligence of the intelligent I will frustrate.' Where is the wise person? Where is the teacher of the law? Where is the philosopher of this age? Has not God made foolish the wisdom of the world? For since in the wisdom of God the world through its wisdom did not know him, God was pleased through the foolishness of what was preached to save those who believe. Jews demand signs and Greeks look for wisdom, but we preach Christ crucified: a stumbling block to Jews and foolishness to Gentiles, but to those whom God has called, both Jews and Greeks, Christ the power of God and the wisdom of God. For the foolishness of God is wiser than human wisdom, and the weakness of God is stronger than human strength. Brothers and sisters, think of what you were when you were called. Not many of you were wise by human standards; not many were influential; not many were of noble birth. But God chose the foolish things of the world to shame the wise; God chose the weak things of the world to shame the strong. God chose the lowly things of this world and the despised things—and the things that are not—to nullify the things that are, so that no one may boast before him. It is because of him that you are in Christ Jesus, who has become for us wisdom from God—that is, our righteousness, holiness and redemption. Therefore, as it is written: 'Let the one who boasts boast in the Lord.'" (1 Corinthians 1:17-31)

---

6 παρέδωκεν in the Greek.

There are vast differences between the wisdom of this age and Godly wisdom. Wisdom which comes from God will be based on the cross of Christ. His wisdom destroys the wisdom of the wise and the intelligence of the intelligent. Christians are dependent on Christ, not on their own reason and strength. Everything that is of value comes from Him. There are an estimated two billion Christians in the world today, but many of those do not hold a consistent, thorough biblical worldview. All Christians are in the process of becoming more like Christ, and therefore are increasingly being conformed to a biblical worldview as they mature in Him. Conversely, secular humanism is not a religion or even a well-defined philosophy. It is a way of thinking which begins with the presupposition that there is no God. If there is no God, then everything has to be explained using non-supernatural means. The Humanist Manifesto II reads, "Humanism is a progressive philosophy of life that, without supernaturalism, affirms our ability and responsibility to lead ethical lives of personal fulfillment that aspire to the greater good of humanity."[7] Humanism is based on wrong ideas of human nature and an erroneous view of history and society. Humanism is a cancer eating away the moral foundation of America.

CATEGORY	SECULAR HUMANISM	BIBLICAL CHRISTIANITY
1. View of God	Atheism	God created and preserves the universe
2. Authority	Man is his own final authority. The individual is autonomous	Man is under God's authority
3. Man's nature	Man is inherently good	Man is inherently sinful
4. Source of problems	Inner disharmony and societal corruption	Sin
5. Primary tool	Human reason	The work of the Holy Spirit and application of God's Word

7 Definition from the *Humanist Manifesto III*, downloadable from www.american humanist.org.

CATEGORY	SECULAR HUMANISM	BIBLICAL CHRISTIANITY
6. Methodology for reform	Getting in touch with our "real self"	Getting in touch with God
7. Ultimate goal	Create a utopian society where every person is self-actualized	Enjoy God forever

This chart shows the differences between a Secular Humanist and a Biblical Christian worldview. We will now look at each of these differences in detail.

1. View of God

Secular humanism assumes that we live in a closed system called naturalism with no creator God and no supernatural causal agent. Thus, we are on our own. What we know is attained through reason alone. Everything can be explained through natural cause and effect. The secular humanism worldview was summarized in two original proclamations called Humanist Manifesto I and Humanist Manifesto II. The first was written in 1933; the second in 1973. There was a third manifesto released in 2003 called Humanism and Its Aspirations. Even though these manifestos had a limited number of signatories, the underlying philosophy of them reflected and has permeated American and Western culture. Humanist Manifesto II says:

> "We believe, however, that traditional dogmatic or authoritarian religions that place revelation, God, ritual, or creed above human needs and experience do a disservice to the human species. Any account of nature should pass the tests of scientific evidence; in our judgment, the dogmas and myths of traditional religions do not do so. Even at this late date in human history, certain elementary facts based upon the critical use of scientific reason have to be restated." It continues, "We can discover no divine purpose or providence for the human species. While

there is much that we do not know, humans are responsible for what we are or will become. No deity will save us; we must save ourselves. Promises of immortal salvation or fear of eternal damnation are both illusory and harmful. They distract humans from present concerns, from self-actualization, and from rectifying social injustices ... As far as we know, the total personality is a function of the biological organism transacting in a social and cultural context. There is no credible evidence that life survives the death of the body."[8]

Humanist Corliss Lamont, in his book *The Philosophy of Humanism*, says, "There is no place in the humanist worldview for either immortality or God in the valid meanings of those terms. Humanism contends that instead of the gods creating the cosmos, the cosmos, in the individualized form of human beings giving reign to their imagination, created the gods."[9]

Character Profile
Noah - Trust in the Lord

God says of Noah that he was a righteous man, blameless among the people of his time (Genesis 6:9). God decided that the Earth had become so corrupt after the fall of man that He was going to have to destroy the Earth and everything on it. Noah, though, found favor with the Lord and God established His covenant with Noah (Genesis 6:18). God instructed Noah to build an ark where he, his family, and male and female pairs of the animals on the Earth would be protected from the waters of the flood. At that time, there had been no rain of any kind on the Earth, so no one had experienced a flood. Noah believed God and built the ark.

---

8 *Humanist Manifesto II.*
9 Lamont, p. 145.

Noah was the prototype of a person who trusted in God. He did exactly what the Lord asked him to do, building the ark to exact specifications. Noah and his family were saved from the flood and became the progenitors of the renewed Earth.

We can trust in the Lord when we trust who He is. The foundation of our walk with Christ is that we trust that God and His character are perfect (Matthew 5:48) and He has called us to be perfect as He is perfect. His character is loving and on our side, merciful, truthful, compassionate, and caring. God is looking for obedience to His leading and His teaching, done out of love for Him (Romans 6:17). If we don't trust Him, we will not obey Him. If we do not know Him, we will not trust Him. As we trust Him, we will desire to be like Him.

Biblical Christianity starts from the premise that there is a God who created and preserves the universe. Christians believe that there is sufficient evidence to prove to anyone that God does exist. The modus operandi is revelation, what God has spoken, not just reason alone. Furthermore, we believe that God is moving the world toward a conclusion where there is a new Heaven and Earth where Jesus Christ, the firstborn of all creation, rules. Colossians 1:16-17 says, "For in him all things were created: things in heaven and on earth, visible and invisible, whether thrones or powers or rulers or authorities; all things have been created through him and for him. He is before all things, and in him all things hold together."

If we place ourselves before God, then we do not rise to moral and philosophical heights and the fulfillment of ideals, but rather we fall into philosophical darkness. God is the only one who can lift us above self-interest and give us a purpose and a new nature to do the things we were designed by Him to achieve. If there is no God, then there is no standard of right and wrong (ethics) and no model to which to aspire (character). There is no perfection of character since there is nothing absolute. If there is a God, however, we have both a model of perfection and a goal to which we can be held accountable.

1 Corinthians 2:11-14 says, "For who knows a person's thoughts except their own spirit within them? In the same way no one knows the thoughts of God except the Spirit of God. What we have received is not the spirit of the world, but the Spirit who is from God, so that we may understand what God has freely given us. This is what we speak, not in words taught us by human wisdom but in words taught by the Spirit, explaining spiritual realities with Spirit-taught words. The person without the Spirit does not accept the things that come from the Spirit of God but considers them foolishness, and cannot understand them because they are discerned only through the Spirit." There is a great divide between those who have the Spirit of God and those who don't. Those without the Spirit of God may have great intellect, but their thinking is natural and they cannot understand the things of God. The great thinkers of today who do not base their thinking on biblical truth will be shown to be the fools of tomorrow. Those who are living in darkness are living under the power of Satan, their minds are darkened, and they have no choice but to stumble around hoping to find some kind of philosophical solid ground on which to stand.

Examined from a biblical worldview, if there is no God, no afterlife, and no judgment, then life is meaningless. The goal of our lives is nothing more than to eat, drink and be merry, to maximize our comfort and happiness. If, however, there is a God as revealed in the Bible, then the best is yet to come. The main problem with humanism and its scientific rationale of evolutionism is that there is no purpose for mankind on earth. If I am descended from an ape, then I might as well live like an ape. Meaning comes from having a relationship with God. We are given worth, dignity, and honor from God; we are created by Him and for Him and are part of His family. "In him we were also chosen, having been predestined according to the plan of him who works out everything in conformity with the purpose of his will, in order that we, who were the first to put our hope in Christ, might be for the praise of his glory." (Ephesians 1:11-12)

> Biblical Christianity starts from the premise that humans are under the authority of God.

Contrary to secular humanism, relationship with the living God does not suppress freedom. Humanist Manifesto II says, "We reject all religious, ideological, or moral codes that denigrate the individual, suppress freedom, dull intellect, and dehumanize personality." Biblical Christianity states that true freedom comes only from Jesus Christ and is the choice to be governed by another force than sinful passions. Freedom is the ability to choose righteousness, since it is righteousness which liberates us from futility and darkness in our understanding.

2. Authority

Secular humanism starts from the premise that man is his own final authority. Humanist Lucia K. B. Hall writes, "Traditional religious belief has assumed that a deity was both the source and enforcer of the only possible right ethical system. As secular humanists, however, we need to discover a naturalistic explanation for the ethical impulse. Since the source of this impulse cannot be found in reason, we need to look to an irrational, emotional response that has evolved as part of the human species."[10] The Humanist Manifesto II adds, "Individuals should be encouraged to realize their own creative talents and desires … We believe in maximum individual autonomy consonant with social responsibility. Although science can account for the causes of behavior, the possibilities of individual freedom of choice exist in human life and should be increased."

Biblical Christianity starts from the premise that humans are under the authority of God. We are not independent agents creating our own rules, but dependent agents who are called to obey God's rules. If God is the authority, and He wrote the Bible which is authoritative, then we are to be subject to what Scripture says. The code of Christian ethics comes from God's revelation in His Word. God created us to enjoy life with Him, but only if we will live a holy and righteous life. American religious leader and writer David A. Noebel says that in humanism, "man is the final judge of right and wrong. But haven't we shown that man is not capable of really deciding right from wrong? Our concept of right and

---

10 Noebel, p. 201.

wrong seems to go with the culture in which we have grown up. If our culture is righteous and moral, then we learn moral ways to approach life. If our culture has been immoral or amoral, then we never learn a moral approach to life."[11] He continues, "Humanists disagree as to what the best consequences of moral actions could be. Should utilitarianism (the greatest good for the greatest number) be considered the measure for the ethical value of an action? Or should we focus on fulfilling our desires? Or should the goal be something more futuristic, such as a global village? And whatever the end-based standard is, why should we pursue that end rather than some other? With no transcendent standard to appeal to, there seems to be no way to answer that question other than a fainthearted, 'Do your own thing,' which amounts to no ethic at all."[12]

If there is no God and there is no standard outside of ourselves, then we are free to live any way that we want as long as we don't interfere with the happiness or well-being of someone else. When we die, we cease to exist and will not be held accountable for what we have or have not done while on this Earth. The only authorities are ourselves and other human beings to whom we submit in this life.

Biblical Christianity maintains, in contrast, that authority is important, and that character is developed in and expressed through relationships of authority—man/God relationships, man/woman relationships, parent/child relationships, and relationships with the governing authorities. Out of authority comes order, and order is essential in society, the church, the home, and the government. American syndicated columnist, pundit, author and radio commentator Cal Thomas says, "The Christian who understands that the world is fallen and that sin's impact infects and affects everything we do recognizes that this is an abnormal world. But the unbeliever sees what surrounds him as normal and tries to bring order, perfection, and hope out of a situation that, from the Christian perspective, is abnormal, imperfect, and hopeless apart from God."[13]

Identified by some with humanism is the idea of "social Darwinism"

---

11 Ibid, p. 201.
12 Ibid, p. 204.
13 Thomas, p. 124.

where the strongest person wins. The strong is often defined by who is most brutal, uncaring about other people, and the one with the best weapons. Historically, the United States of America has been both a strong and a good nation, unusual among the world's empires. This is because it has had Judeo-Christian values and a Judeo-Christian world-view as its foundation.[14] Power has to be combined with goodness, virtue, righteousness, and compassion to be godly. Jesus paved the way as one who was both powerful and good. In God's order, it is the humble, the meek, and the righteous who rule (Matthew 5:1-10).

3. Man's nature

Secular humanism states that people are inherently good and the Humanist does not view human beings as fallen. Humanist psychologist Carl Rogers says, "I see members of the human species, like members of other species, as essentially constructive in their fundamental nature, but damaged by their experience."[15] "For myself, though I am very well aware of the incredible amount of destructive, cruel, malevolent behavior in today's world—from the threats of war to the senseless violence in the street—I do not find that this evil is inherent in human nature."[16] German social psychologist, sociologist and humanistic philosopher Erich Fromm adds, "The position taken by humanistic ethics that man is able to know what is good and to act accordingly on the strength of his natural potentialities and of his reason would be untenable if the dogma of man's innate natural evilness were true."[17] The intellectually consistent secular humanist does not believe that mind and spirit exist. The mind is just autonomic responses. Every decision made by humans should be nothing more than the natural results of synapses firing in the brain. Humanistic psychology is based on the theory of self-actualization, the full realization of one's

---

14 Of course, the history of our country is replete with ungodly men and women, but most of the founders of our Constitution and Bill of Rights were either Christians or Deists. For an explanation of this assertion, consult the 10 part video series *The American Heritage Series*, put out by *Wallbuilders* and featuring Dr. David Barton.

15 Noebel, p. 359.

16 Ibid, p. 355.

17 Ibid, p. 359.

potential. American psychologist Abraham Maslow further developed the theory of self-actualization, saying that human creative potential is released when physiological, safety, love and belonging, and esteem needs are satisfied. People who have reached self-actualization are characterized by certain behaviors, such as:

- They embrace reality and facts rather than denying truth.
- They are spontaneous.
- They are interested in solving problems.
- They are accepting of themselves and others and lack prejudice.

Maslow defined self-actualization as the desire to become more and more what one is, to become everything that one is capable of becoming.[18] He did not feel that self-actualization determined one's life; rather, he felt that it gave the individual motivation to achieve budding ambitions. "As far as I know, we just don't have any intrinsic instincts for evil," he said. "If you think in terms of the basic needs; instincts, at least at the outset, are all 'good'—or perhaps we should be technical about it and call them 'pre-moral', neither good nor evil."[19] Humanist Wendell W. Waters added, "The true Christian is running furiously on a treadmill to get away from whole segments of his or her human nature which he or she is taught to fear or about which he or she is taught to feel guilty. The Christian is brainwashed to believe that he or she was born wicked, should suffer as Christ suffered, and should aspire to a humanly impossible level of perfection nonetheless." He continues, "A true Christian must always be in a state of torment, since he or she can never really be certain that God has forgiven him or her for deeply felt negative feelings—in spite of the Catholic confessional and the fundamentalist trick of self-deception known as being saved or born again."[20]

Part of secular humanism philosophy is the "human potential movement." It arose out of the milieu of the 1960s and formed around the concept of cultivating extraordinary potential that its advocates

18 Wikipedia article on "Maslow".
19 Maslow, Abraham. *Humanistic Psychology*, ed. Welch, Tate, and Richards, p. 32.
20 Noebel, p. 360.

believed to lie largely untapped in all people. The movement took as its premise the belief that through the development of human potential, humans can experience an exceptional quality of life filled with happiness, creativity, and fulfillment. As a corollary, those who begin to unleash this assumed potential often find themselves directing their actions within society towards assisting others to release their potential. Adherents believe that the net effect of individuals cultivating their potential will bring about positive social change at large. The movement has its conceptual roots in existentialism and humanism. Its emergence is linked to humanistic psychology, also known as the "third force" in psychology (after psychoanalysis and behaviorism, and before the "fourth force" of transpersonal psychology—which emphasizes esoteric, psychic, mystical, and spiritual development).[21] The human potential movement and humanistic therapy is distinguished by the following emphases:

- A concern for what is uniquely human rather than what humans share with other animals.
- A focus on each person's open-ended growth rather than reshaping individuals to fit society's demands.
- An interest in the here-and-now rather than in a person's childhood history or supposed unconscious conflicts.
- A holistic approach concerned with all levels of human being and functioning—not just the intellectual—including creative and spiritual functioning.
- A focus on psychological health rather than disturbance.[22]

In contrast, biblical Christianity starts from the premise that people have a sinful nature, which doesn't mean that everything we do and think is wrong, but rather that every part of us is tainted with sin; therefore, we cannot have a relationship with God unless and until the issue of sin is dealt with through the blood of Christ. Romans 3:10-12 says, "There is no one righteous, not even one; there is no one who understands; there is

---

21 Wikipedia article on the "Human Potential movement."
22 Website: http://medical-dictionary.thefreedictionary.com/Human-Potential+Movement.

no one who seeks God. All have turned away, they have together become worthless; there is no one who does good, not even one."

Biblical Christianity teaches that guilt is objective, not subjective. We stand guilty before God and we need to have an answer for the guilt—the ransom of Christ for our sin so that we will not have any more guilt. Much of the emphasis of modern humanistic psychology has been on getting us to feel good about ourselves. It is not a matter of *feeling* good but of *being* good. That only happens through a relationship with Christ. In addition, biblical Christianity states that people are not perfectible by their own efforts, but only by the transforming work of God's Holy Spirit. We can reach our human potential only through transformation, not reformation. It is not a matter of trying harder, but of receiving a new nature. For example, the Bible starts from the premise that foolishness is bound in the heart of a child and that children are to be trained into righteousness. Secular humanism emphasizes bringing out the inner goodness, creativity, and uniqueness of the child. The assumption for humanists is that the child has everything it needs to develop, if someone simply finds the means to tap into their inner being.

If there is no sin nature, then we are able to reform ourselves. If, however, we have a sin nature, then we are incapable of doing what is right. We want to become good, but we find ourselves unable. Romans 7:18-23 says, "For I know that good itself does not dwell in me, that is, in my sinful nature. For I have the desire to do what is good, but I cannot carry it out. For I do not do the good I want to do, but the evil I do not want to do—this I keep on doing. Now if I do what I do not want to do, it is no longer I who do it, but it is sin living in me that does it. So I find this law at work: Although I want to do good, evil is right there with me. For in my inner being I delight in God's law; but I see another law at work in me, waging war against the law of my mind and making me a prisoner of the law of sin at work within me."

> We are to let God guide our life, not our natural inclinations that will lead us astray

Christians are commanded in the Bible to put off the old man and put on the new man. The goal is not to express the inner man or some-how bring out its natural goodness, but to suppress it, deny it, and put it to death. Likewise, we are to let God guide our life, not our natural incli-nations that will lead us astray. We are to deny ourselves, not encourage self-centeredness and self-absorption. Real joy is found in humbling our-selves and giving to others. The deception of humanistic psychology and self-actualization lies in the teaching that we help others by helping our-selves. Jesus came in order to make it possible to be Christ-centered and other-centered instead of being focused on self.

Finally, the goal of the Christian life is not self-actualization, but serving God; not maximizing our potential, but maximizing God's pres-ence on Earth. Our potential, however, is REALIZED FOR HIS GLORY as we serve God. He will bring us to the place of maximum usefulness. It is to God's glory that we become useful. Christians believe in an eternal God who provides eternal life with eternal rewards.

4. Source of problems

Secular humanism takes inner disharmony and societal corruption as the source of mankind's problems. The humanist believes that people are essentially good, so there has to be an explanation given for why we see so much evil in the world. Society and its institutions are responsi-ble for the evil acts of people. Maslow said, "Sick people are made by a sick culture; healthy people are made possible by a healthy culture."[23] Emphasis shifts from individual responsibility for our actions to insti-tutional responsibility, usually the government. If we can eliminate poverty and income inequality, we can work toward a culture which produces healthy individuals. Humanist Lawrence Frank says: "The 'evil' in man becomes increasingly explicable as a product of what is done to and for the child and youth who, faced with these threats, these humiliations and denials, attempts to protect and maintain himself by distorted patterns of belief, action, and feeling. These dis-turbances of personality appear, like disease, to be the efforts of the

---

23 Noebel, p. 361.

organism-personality to maintain itself in the face of a menacing environment, efforts that may be self-destructive as well as anti-social."[24]

I was educated in secular schools through a master's program in economics. I was fully convinced that men were good by nature and that the way to deal with problems was to reform society. I studied psychology in order to find some of the answers, but I began to be increasingly uncomfortable with what I was finding. I remember one experiment in particular where people were told that they were testing the limits of human suffering. Subjects were given control on how much pain they could induce in subjects as they had electricity passed through them. The people in the experiment were told how much to turn the dial. The experiment was intended to see how far people would go in obeying authority. Many of the people went as far as turning the dial until the person strapped to the chair was seemingly screaming out in pain and then slumped over from the electricity sent through their body. It showed me the depths of human depravity. I also saw in history the depths of human sin. There is no other explanation for some of the things which have taken place historically—the holocaust, world wars, gang wars, white collar crime, hatred, brutality, and all the other things which make it very difficult to believe that man is basically good. The emergence of the brutality through ISIS has reconfirmed that mankind is not good. We have seen a brutality which we thought was relegated to the distant past.

Biblical Christianity states that sin is the source of mankind's problems. The problem is not with culture, systems, or society—but with the people in the society. There is no perfect society because there are no perfect people. Society does corrupt people, but people also corrupt society. The United States of America was founded on the principle that men are inherently sinful. Balances (the three branches of government) were built into the U.S. Constitution as a check upon the abuse of any one person. The United States government has worked very well over the years because it was founded not upon utopian dreams, but the biblical principle of the sinfulness of men.

---

24 Lawrence K. Frank, "Potentialities of Human Nature," *The Humanist*, April 1951, p. 65. Quoted in *Understanding the Times*, p. 361.

A lack of Christian character cannot be blamed on the corruption of society. Talk show host Dennis Prager says moral character begins "with taking care of oneself, if one is able to. Conversely, it is a moral defect to rely on others when one does not have to ... The more the state takes care of its citizens, the more deleterious the effects are on most citizens' moral character ... The essence of good character is to be a responsible person, meaning first and foremost, taking responsibility for oneself."[25] Biblical Christianity deals head-on with personal responsibility. We are responsible before God and we are responsible for our own actions. We always have the choice to do what is right in God's eyes. Prager adds, "When it comes to personal relations and, even more so, to formulating social policy, intending to do good is completely insufficient. In order to do good in both the personal and social spheres, people also need wisdom, common sense, and a moral value system."[26] I am convinced that many of those who don't believe in the sinfulness of man have good intentions of creating a better society which produces better people. The problem is that they will be frustrated. Better systems with the same unredeemed people will simply lead to the corruption of those systems. Poor systems with good people will move toward becoming better systems.

Historically, Christians have been at the forefront of helping to solve many of the injustices of the world—such as equality of women, health care, child labor, abolition of slavery, and prostitution.[27] Christ came to bring justice to the world, but He knew that the issue of human sin had to be dealt with first. Out of a renewed heart comes a renewed interest and passion for being involved in helping to cure injustice in the world. Self-centered, sinful people will not be the catalyst for societal change. Sinful man needs God to make a moral society. I'm not saying that non-Christians never do anything good and that every Christian does only good things, but I am saying that sanctification has to come after redemption. We have to get the order right—first deal with our own sinful nature, then focus

---

25 Prager, location 5225.
26 Prager, location 1232.
27 For a detailed explanation of the role of Christianity in helping to solve injustice in the world, see Alvin J. Schmidt's *How Christianity Changed the World*.

on society. In addition, if Christians help people to live a better life but don't introduce them to eternal life, then we are giving them only part of the solution; the lesser part. "For whoever wants to save their life will lose it, but whoever loses their life for me and for the gospel will save it. What good is it for someone to gain the whole world, yet forfeit their soul? Or what can anyone give in exchange for their soul? (Mark 8:35-37)

5. Primary tool

Secular humanism takes human reason as the fundamental tool for discovering what is right and what is wrong, what is ethical and what is not. Humanist Manifesto II says, "Reason and intelligence are the most effective instruments that humankind possesses. There is no substitute: neither faith nor passion suffices in itself. Man himself, with no tools but the power and objectivity of his reason, can assemble a true and accurate vision of himself and his world, and he can interpret that vision. Man himself, totally apart from God or supernatural revelation, can not only solve his personal problems and those of the world, but he can actually make himself and his world a better place to live in."[28]

Biblical Christianity states that we cannot change ourselves and we need more than human effort to see genuine inner transformation. We are incapable of our own redemption, our own sanctification, and our own glorification. Biblical Christianity begins with revelation, illumination, and application of God's Word through the sanctifying work of His Holy Spirit in order to arrive at truth. God's principles are already given; we only need to interpret and apply them to particular situations. Christians use reason to discover who God is, not to come up with explanations which leave God out of the picture. We are exhorted to be renewed in our minds so that we begin to think the way that God thinks. If we want goodness to prevail, a relationship with God and application of His wisdom is the key to making it happen.

6. Methodology for reform

---

28 *Humanist Manifesto II*, section on ethics.

Secular humanism asserts that mental health can be restored to everyone who gets in touch with his real "good" self. Humanists believe that truly free men will be able to get in touch with their inherent perfection and create a utopian world civilization.

Humanist Manifesto I says, "Religious humanism considers the complete realization of human personality to be the end of man's life and seeks its develop-

> God created us and only He knows what we need in order to be emotionally healthy.

ment and fulfillment in the here and now.[29] The task of the humanistic psychologist, then, is simply to unlock the potential creativity and goodness inherent in every human being. Mental health can be achieved worldwide, as soon as each individual's self-actualization needs are met. Specifically, as soon as each individual learns to love and nurture his real self, the mission of humanism will be fulfilled."[30]

Humanist Manifesto II adds, "We appreciate the need to preserve the best ethical teachings in the religious traditions of humankind, many of which we share in common. But we reject those features of traditional religious morality that deny humans a full appreciation of their own potentialities and responsibilities. Traditional religions often offer solace to humans, but as often they inhibit humans from helping themselves or experiencing their full potentialities. Such institutions, creeds, and rituals often impede the will to serve others. Too often traditional faiths encourage dependence rather than independence, obedience rather than affirmation, fear rather than courage."[31] We as Christians believe that rather than inhibiting our potential, it is only God who can actualize our potential. Only He understands who we are deep inside. At the fall man lost touch with who he really is, and only God knows what our full potential is, that which we had before the fall. Our potential is only realized as we deal with the sin in our lives; it is sin which limits our potential. We cannot really be affirmed until we are affirmed by God, since He is the one who made us. Furthermore, only God can

---

29 *Humanist Manifesto I* can be downloaded at www.americanhumanist.org.
30 Noebel, 365.
31 *Humanist Manifesto II*, section on religion.

give us courage to press forward and become what we were intended to be. So, rather than a relationship with Christ becoming a ball and chain around our ankles, our relationship with God is our set of wings to set us free to be everything which we were intended to be.

Humanists believe that self-actualization is achieved when the individual achieves full development of his or her abilities and ambitions.[32] The main problem, they believe, is that few people are in touch with their real selves, and do not love themselves enough. "Since this inner nature is good or neutral rather than bad," Maslow said, "it is best to bring it out and to encourage it rather than to suppress it. If it is permitted to guide our life, we grow healthy, fruitful, and happy."[33] Once an individual becomes self-actualized, he will be capable of acting in harmony with his true self, and his true self always desires good. Therefore, the man who listens to his real inner nature will always act morally.[34] Erich Fromm adds, "I shall attempt to show that the character structure of the mature and integrated personality, the productive character, constitutes the source and basis of 'virtue,' and that 'vice,' in the last analysis, is indifference to one's own self and self-mutilation. Not self-renunciation nor selfishness but the affirmation of his truly human self is the supreme value of humanistic ethics. If man is to have confidence in values, he must know himself and the capacity of his nature for goodness and productiveness."[35]

Biblical Christianity states that we cannot look within and find mental health, since we cannot be integrated unless we are in touch with God and are sacrificing our lives for someone else. God created us and only He knows what we need in order to be emotionally healthy. Emotional health begins with spiritual health—which begins with a right relationship with God. This does not mean that everyone who has a personal relationship with God through Jesus Christ is emotionally healthy, but it does mean that spiritual health is the beginning place for emotional health, and that seeking emotional health without spiritual health is unhealthy. Author

32 Noebel, p. 364.

33 Noebel, p. 362, quoting Maslow, *Toward a Psychology of Being*, p. 4.

34 Ibid, p. 366.

35 Fromm, *Man for Himself*, p. 17. Quoted in Noebel, p. 367

Peter Scazzero says that God's image includes physical, spiritual, emotional, intellectual, and social dimensions. "Ignoring any aspect of who we are as men and women made in God's image always results in destructive consequences in our relationship with God, with others, and with ourselves."[36] When we try to define maturity without all these dimensions, we end up with a truncated maturity. Only in the balance of these different dimensions do we come into genuine wholeness and maturity.

Oswald Chambers said, "Our Lord's teaching was always anti-self-realization. His purpose is not the development of a person—His purpose is to make a person exactly like Himself, and the Son of God is characterized by self-expenditure. If we believe in Jesus, it is not what we gain but what He pours through us that really counts. God's purpose is not simply to make us beautiful, plump grapes, but to make us grapes so that He may squeeze the sweetness out of us."[37] Self-actualization is developed in healthy environments. A healthy church, a healthy family, and a healthy school will be the place where children grow up emotionally and spiritually healthy. Human potential is developed in a healthy environment where there is love, acceptance, and intellectual stimulation—an environment of grace.

7. Ultimate goal

Secular humanism seeks to create a utopian society in which inequality among classes of people is abolished and there is material or economic equality in the world. This utopian society takes place when humanity is no longer divided along nationalistic grounds, but under a transnational federal government. Humanist Manifesto II says, "We deplore the division of humankind on nationalistic grounds. We have reached a turning point in human history where the best option is to transcend the limits of national sovereignty and to move toward the building of a world community in which all sectors of the human family can participate. Thus we look to the development of a system of world law and a world order based

36 Scazzero, p. 18.
37 *My Utmost*, Sept 2.

upon transnational federal government. This would appreciate cultural pluralism and diversity. It would not exclude pride in national origins and accomplishments nor the handling of regional problems on a regional basis. Human progress, however, can no longer be achieved by focusing on one section of the world, Western or Eastern, developed or underdeveloped. For the first time in human history, no part of humankind can be isolated from any other. Each person's future is in some way linked to all. We thus reaffirm a commitment to the building of world community, at the same time recognizing that this commits us to some hard choices."[38]

Character Profile
David - Humility

Saul was king over Israel. David had defeated the Philistine Goliath and cut off his head. The Philistine warriors ran for their lives and the Israelites ran after them all the way back to Philistia, killing the Philistines as they pursued them. Saul had promised that whoever killed Goliath would be given great wealth, an exemption for his father's family from taxes, and Saul's daughter in marriage. When the Israelites returned from battle, the women came out from the towns, dancing and singing "Saul has slain his thousands, and David his tens of thousands." Saul became jealous of David, but he couldn't kill him outright because everyone in Israel and Judah loved David and everything David did was successful. At first, Saul pledged his daughter Merab to David, but later gave her to another man. When Saul saw that his daughter Michal was in love with David, he told David he could have her if he brought Saul two hundred foreskins of Philistine men. David replied, "Who am I, and what is my family or my clan in Israel, that I should become the king's son-in-law?"(1 Samuel 18:18) Again, David said, "Do you think it is a small matter to become the king's son-in-law? I am only a poor man and little known." (1 Samuel 18:23)

David's humility was the foundation of his character, and humil-

---

38 *Humanist Manifesto II*, section on world community.

ity should also be the foundation of our character. Humility is the starting place for character formation. With humility comes wisdom, honor, and the ability to grow in Christ. If we have genuine humility, we will be open to hearing from God and walking with Him. The Bible states that we are to humble ourselves. Seek humility in your Christian walk and God will bless you richly.

Biblical Christianity teaches that people are sinners. Therefore, centralization of power in a transnational government will lead to more concentrated power in the hands of one or a few people. Power corrupts and absolute power corrupts absolutely. Christians have a profound distrust of the goodness of man. "Much, perhaps even most, evil does not emanate from particularly evil people or even from the bad or self-centered parts of human nature," Prager says, "but from the good and idealistic parts."[39] Novelist and theologian C.S. Lewis wrote, "The greatest evil is not done in those sordid 'dens of crime' that Dickens loved to paint ... it is conceived and ... moved, seconded, carried, and minuted ... in clean, carpeted, warmed, and well-lighted offices, by quiet men with white collars and cut fingernails and smooth-shaven cheeks who do not need to raise their voices."[40] Jesus did not seek to establish an earthly kingdom, but rather He came to bring the Kingdom of God to Earth. The Pharisees sent some of their disciples to Jesus to ask Him whether or not it was right to pay taxes to Caesar or not. Jesus had them show Him the coin used to pay the taxes. He then replied, "Give to Caesar what is Caesar's, and to God what is God's." (Matthew 22:21) Jesus had many opportunities to establish a kingdom on Earth, but His mission here was not to come as the conquering king, but as the sin bearer. He will come as the conquering king, but only at the end of time. Men trying to establish utopia without dealing with sin in the human heart is futile. Utopia will only come when Christ is reigning as King.

---

39 Prager, location 1217.
40 Colson, *Against the Night*, p. 46.

Post-modernism and New Age psychology

We will now turn our attention to what is called Post-modernism or the New Age movement. Post-modernism is increasingly influencing modernism and secular humanism and is primarily expressed through the New Age movement, described as an extremely large meta-network of people and groups who share common values and a common vision. These values are based in Eastern/occult mysticism and pantheistic monism (the worldview that all is one, and this one is God) and the vision is of a coming era of peace and enlightenment, the Age of Aquarius. It has become a third major social force vying with traditional Judeo-Christian religion and secular humanism for cultural dominance. It represents an historical movement that can be traced over a period of more than two centuries in the West from orthodox Christianity back to paganism—fitting, since the New Age movement is a resurgence of paganism. It is the occult going public after centuries of hiding itself at the cultural periphery. There are no centralized organizations controlling doctrines, activities, or agendas. It is a leaderless but powerful network found in every facet of American society. Within the New Age movement are the consciousness movement, the holistic health movement, the human potential movement, followers of many Eastern gurus and Western occult, and metaphysical teachers.

The New Age movement is born out of dissatisfaction with Western society's answers to the problems we face. It is a rejection of mainstream Western values and institutions. It is an attempt to revolutionize every facet of life on personal, interpersonal, societal, and global scales. New Agers tend to be eclectic: they draw what they think is the best from many sources. Long-term, exclusive devotion to a single teacher, teaching, or technique is not the norm. The New Age Journal says, "The many issues of the new consciousness are like peanuts: You can't eat just one. The stockbroker, for example, who began dabbling in alternative body therapies ten years ago has quite probably gone on to the likes of meditation or the ecology movement or Zen studies by now, and no doubt he notices the aperture in his personal cosmic egg getting wider all the time."[41]

---

41 *Crash Course*, p. 16.

Randall N. Baer, a former leader in the New Age movement and now a Christian, says in his book *Inside the New Age Nightmare*: "Essentially, it is a Satan-controlled, modern-day mass revival of occult-based philosophies and practices in both obvious and cleverly disguised forms."[42] Marilyn Ferguson, who wrote the landmark book about the New Age movement entitled *The Aquarian Conspiracy: Personal and Social Transformation in the 1980s*, says "broader than reform, deeper than revolution, this benign conspiracy for a new human agenda has triggered the most rapid cultural realignment in history. This great shuddering, irrevocable shift overtaking us is not a new political, religious, philosophical system. It is a new mind—the ascendance of a startling worldview."[43]

It was not until late in 1986 and throughout 1987 that the New Age movement finally caught the media's attention in America when actress Shirley MacLaine emerged as the movement's unofficial but recognized spokeswoman. Many of its basic beliefs come from India and its Eastern swamis and gurus. There are some basic differences between Indian Hinduism and the American version. Hinduism is world-denying. The world is illusion and considered to be a formidable obstacle to eternal bliss. Those who are serious about seeking God and salvation are expected to renounce the world of temporal pleasures and responsibilities. In America, New Agers affirm the value of temporal realities: people, nature, culture, education, politics, even science and technology. Proponents try to graft the fruits of higher learning onto the various branches of mystical tradition. They want to change the world, not drop out of it. They desire personal (earthly) as well as spiritual fulfillment. Baer says the movement "has already enlisted the minds, hearts, and resources of some of our most advanced thinkers, including Nobel laureate scientists, philosophers, statesmen, celebrities, and steadily growing numbers from every corner of American society. The network is working to create a different kind of society based on a vastly enlarged concept of human

---

42 Baer, p. 78.
43 Ibid., p. 80.

potential [and] shows us how the technologies for expanding and transforming personal consciousness, once the secret of an elite, are now generating massive change in every cultural institution—medicine, politics, business, education, religions, and the family."[44]

There are an estimated twelve million New Agers in America, though some put the figure as high as 60 million. Tucson, Arizona is one of the hubs of the New Age movement along with Sedona, Arizona and Santa Fe, New Mexico. Business corporations (including numerous Fortune 500 companies) spend $4 billion on management and employee programs that subtly but distinctly are based on New Age philosophies and practices. There are over 200,000 registered witches in America. Untold numbers are unregistered. Jean Houston, Ph.D., one of the most renowned New Age leaders, reports having led a three-day intensive workshop for 150 high-ranking government officials, and other workshops included top-level corporate businessmen and government officials.[45] Professor Carl Raschke, a New Age critic, calls this movement "the most powerful social force in the country today." He adds, "If you look at it carefully you see that it represents a complete rejection of Judeo-Christian and bedrock American values."[46]

> New Agers are pantheists. Everything that exists is God.

New Agers are pantheists. Everything that exists is God. Stars are God, water is God, plants are God, trees are God, the Earth is God, whales and dolphins are God, *everything* is God. There is no difference between the creator and the creation. Everything has divine power in it. Their philosophy is non-naturalism; there is nothing natural, all is supernatural. The spiritual dimension of life is most important. New Age writer Ruth Montgomery says, "We are as much God as God is a part of us ... each of us is God ... together we are God ... this all-for-one-and-one-for-all ... makes us the whole of God."[47] Meher Baba, an

---

44 Baer, p. 80.
45 Ibid., p. 81.
46 Ibid., p. 82.
47 Quoted in *Understanding the Times*, p. 851.

Indian spiritual master, says "There is only one question. And once you know the answer to that question there are no more to ask ...Who am I? And to that question there is only one answer—I am God!"[48] Douglas Groothius quotes Swami Muktananda as saying, "Kneel to your own self. Honor and worship your own being. God dwells within you as You."[49] Fritjof Capra says in his book *The Turning Point* that "the ultimate state of consciousness is one in which all boundaries and dualisms have been transcended and all individuality dissolves into universal, undifferentiated oneness."[50] Baer categorizes the New Age as New Age spiritual humanism. "New Age man, believing himself to be divinely perfect and ultimately all-powerful, sets himself up on a cosmic throne. This highly touted god-man claims to have inherently unlimited powers to command and manipulate the universe according to his sovereign will. Man is elevated to divinity, deity, and sovereignty—the essence of the New Age spiritual humanism that seeks to exalt sinful man to godhood and to displace Jesus Christ as King of kings and Lord of lords."[51]

There are a variety of techniques for altering the consciousness and tapping universal energy too numerous to mention here. New Agers consider spirituality much more a matter of experience than belief. Any teaching or technique that facilitates experience is welcome, but there is no loyalty to a rigid, elaborate system of belief. New Agers reject naturalistic and materialistic philosophies. If every aspect of existence is sacred, then everything must have a spiritual nature. And since it is the spiritual side of life that leads to higher consciousness and inner truth, we should view all reality from a supernatural perspective. The spiritual dimension of everything is the important, god-like side of reality. Planet Earth—indeed, the whole universe—is an actual living organism.

New Agers believe in reincarnation and karma. Whatever a person

---

48 Ibid.
49 Groothius, p. 21.
50 Ibid., p. 19.
51 Baer, p. 84.

does in this life will return to him experientially in an exact proportion of good or bad. Since most people are unable to experience all of the bad karma that they have accumulated in one lifetime, they are compelled to return in new incarnations until all of their bad karma has been balanced by good karma. Salvation, then, is a matter of works. Jesus is looked on by New Agers as one of a select company, having achieved Christ consciousness. "Christ" refers to a divine principle within all men. Jesus simply attained consciousness of it. The New Age Jesus became "the Christ" only after purifying himself of bad karma through many incarnations. He is only one of several masters who serve humanity from a higher plane. New Age belief embraces neither theism nor atheism and allows no special revelation. Christ's life was important only in the sense that it showed man to be capable of achieving perfection, even godhood.

Johanna Michaelsen, author of the book *The Beautiful Side of Evil*, said the New Age "is the ultimate eclectic religion of self: Whatever you decide is right for you is what's right, as long as you don't get narrow-minded and exclusive about it."[52] The New Age movement can be described as secular humanism + the supernatural (the occult). Since everything is relative, and there is no absolute truth, there can be no sin. Every person is an island unto himself. Evil is simply ignorance of one's true potential and a frustration of the natural drive toward self-actualization. The self is a sacrosanct island of value. The inherent wisdom and goodness of the self (or any part thereof) is a self-evident truth, almost a metaphysical first principle. Evil is not the product of social factors, but more as a failure to actualize potential or the frustration occurring when the self begins to develop.

New Agers say that we must all tap into our collective unconscious (altered states). We must begin to live and rule our lives as gods. Man is separate from God only in his consciousness. Thus, man needs to bring about an altered state of consciousness. David Spangler, who has been described as the "Emerson of the New Age," says, "We can take all the scriptures, and all the teachings, and all the tablets, and all the laws, and

---

52 Noebel, p. 850.

all the marshmallows and have a jolly good bonfire and marshmallow roast, because that is all they are worth."[53]

New Agers try to find enlightenment through a variety of means: channeling, acquiring familiar spirits, opening up to demonic forces, nature religions, mystical beliefs of the Indian, neo-paganism, sorcerers, goddess worship, witchcraft, and New Age feminism. New Agers typically embrace wiccan traditions and practices like the celebration of eight yearly solar Sabbats, lunar Esbats, and small groups (covens). Other methods include initiations into cosmic mysteries and powers, holistic health, and crystals. More than three-quarter of New Agers firmly believe in the existence of hosts of alien beings within and around planet Earth to assist in the birthing of the New Age.

How does New Age teaching impact teaching about Christian character?

1. We, as biblical Christians, believe that man is sinful. The New Age philosophy teaches that man is born good and is capable of attaining a higher consciousness.

2. The spiritual source of the New Age movement is Satan, not God. There is a denial of God as a person, and there is acceptance of a type of godness in human beings. God is not a person, but rather a spiritual force.

3. It is a welcome thing for the New Ager to correct the naturalistic bent of the secular humanist, to admit that there are spiritual forces in the universe. However, spirituality without Christ is merely opening up to demonic spirits. The spiritual realm is dangerous without the Holy Spirit. The New Age is steeped in the occult, open to the influence and domination of evil spirits.

4. The New Age teaches that we as human beings are the locus of truth and enlightenment. We, as biblical Christians, believe that only God is the locus of truth and enlightenment, and that we as humans are to worship God and accept His Word as truth.

---

53 Ibid., p. 851.

5. Reincarnation is not a biblical principle. We believe that we get only one life on this Earth.

6. The pursuit of cosmic consciousness without Christ's thoughts and direction is illusory and will lead us only into to be influenced by Satan. We cannot achieve "Christ-consciousness" without Christ. Only Christ within can reveal who Christ is. God's thoughts are not our thoughts. To tap into a cosmic consciousness can only lead us downward, not upward; not into unity, but into barbarism; not into enlightenment, but into further depravity.

7. In the New Age movement there is no external standard of righteousness or Christian character. If truth, authority, and all reality is found within us, then there is no need to look beyond ourselves for a standard or model for right living. If there is no right and wrong, then the quest for character outside of ourselves is no longer needed. All that is needed is to look within and you will find God. For a New Ager, then, there is no need for developing character or righteousness or wisdom, since we already have all that we need if we just get in touch with our real self. The distinction between good and evil is hopelessly blurred.

8. Since there is no concept of sin in New Age teaching, there is no concept of salvation. Salvation is self-salvation, achieved through our own efforts, not through the sacrifice of Christ. If there is no sin, then there is no need for redemption through a Savior. We can do it all by ourselves by merely looking within ourselves. The New Age movement takes the concept of self-actualization and adds a supernatural dimension to it.

9. We are not gods. New Agers are trying to take glory away from God and put it on themselves.

10. The New Age philosophy teaches that utopia can be achieved if enough of us achieve cosmic-consciousness and that through our effort the New Age will be ushered in. We believe that only Christ can usher in utopia.

11. The New Age movement introduces a new worldview, but one which is still anti-Christian.

12. Accountability for the New Ager is only to themselves, not to God. There is no outside authority, no one to whom we must give account at the end of the age.

Vital conclusions

1. We have contrasted a biblical worldview with a secular humanistic worldview with respect to their view of God, authority, man's nature, the source of our problems, the primary tool which we use in life, the methodology for reform, and the ultimate goal of the world. Secular humanism and the New Age movement are diametrically opposed to Christian theology and practice. Because a secular humanist worldview and a biblical Christianity worldview begin in different places, they end up in totally different places theologically. The quest for Christian character must begin with the existence of God, with moral absolutes, with the sinfulness of man, with absolute truth as found in the Bible, with the forgiveness of sin and a new nature through the new birth, with the Kingdom of God coming to Earth, and with Jesus Christ reigning in eternity.

2. Our American culture is rapidly moving in the opposite direction from a biblical worldview. If we set out to drive from Chicago to New York and instead take the road toward San Francisco, driving faster toward San Francisco is not going to help us get to New York. The faster we head west, the faster we are going away from our goal. To head away from a belief in God and from a desire to please Him with our lives is really no progress at all, but is actually taking us further from the fullness of life we truly desire. Both secular humanism and New Age philosophy promise what they cannot produce. "Blessed is the one," Psalm 1:1-3 says, "who does not walk in step with the wicked or stand in the way that sinners take or sit in the company of mockers, but whose delight is in the law of the Lord, and who meditates on his law day and night. That person is like a tree planted by streams of water, which yields its fruit in season and whose leaf does not wither—whatever they do prospers." If we want to see fruit from our lives and prosper even in the difficult times, we are to avoid walking with those who live ungodly lives and instead delight in and meditate on God's Word.

QUESTIONS, EXERCISES

1. What do you intend to do differently in your life as a result of seeing the contrast in this chapter between a biblical worldview and a secular humanist or New Age worldview?

2. What are you doing in your life to replace ungodly thinking with godly thinking, based on a biblical worldview?

3. Christianity is cross cultural. What evidences have you seen recently of a cultural war going on in your world?

4. How are you intentionally growing spiritually in your life?

5. 1 John 2:15 says, "Do not love the world or anything in the world. If anyone loves the world, love for the Father is not in them." In what ways can you love people and yet not love the world?

6. James 1:27 says that "religion that God our Father accepts as pure and faultless is this: to look after orphans and widows in their distress and to keep oneself from being polluted by the world." Practically speaking, how can you keep yourself from being polluted by the world?

COMPLETE
THE QUEST

Back in the late 1960s, one of my friends decided he wanted to become more spiritual. He wasn't a Christian, but he was part of the hippie movement in northern California. He trekked into the Sierra Madre mountains for two months in an effort to "commune" with God. He claimed to feel close to God during his time in the woods. However, after coming down from the mountain, he walked into a small grocery store—and it turned his spiritual high on its head. He had experienced such peacefulness and tranquility while alone by himself, but when confronted with real life, the 'spiritual high' bubble burst. He experienced a sense of peace away from contact with other human beings, but had yet to learn that true spirituality is experienced dealing with other people in the nitty-gritty of life. Later, that same friend found in the person of Jesus Christ what he had looked for in the mountains, and it was that very friend who led me to Christ a short while afterward.

As Christians, our theology becomes reality when we live out our daily lives and interact with other people. Jesus' ministry was spent with people. He withdrew to the hills for seasons of prayer, but most of the time He was with the crowds or with His disciples. It's interesting that nobody ever accused Him of hypocrisy, even His disciples who were with Him every day for three years. Why was that? Jesus personified godly character. His theology was made reality in how He lived—and so is ours.

> Christian character is the foundation for everything we do in our lives.

Christian character is the foundation for everything we do in our lives. Everything comes down to what we are on the inside. Even more, if our religion does not penetrate down to the way we treat others and live out our daily lives, it is shallow and we have not allowed Christ to transform us from the inside out by being born again in Him. We cannot merely copy Christian behavior, ignore our theology, and expect to become Christ-like and exhibit Christian character like He did. Why is this quest for Christian character worth everything?

1. Transformation is integral to the life Jesus envisioned

We were designed by God to live a transformed life in which Christ's image is increasingly being manifested in our whole being. In Luke 9:23-26, Jesus said those who wish to be His disciple "must deny themselves and take up their cross daily and follow me. For whoever wants to save their life will lose it, but whoever loses their life for me will save it. What good is it for someone to gain the whole world, and yet lose or forfeit their very self? Whoever is ashamed of me and my words, the Son of Man will be ashamed of them when he comes in his glory and in the glory of the Father and of the holy angels." He later states in Luke 14:26 that "if anyone comes to me and does not hate [that is, love less] father and mother, wife and children, brothers and sisters—yes, even their own life—such a person cannot be my disciple."

Jesus has to be number one in our lives. If we place even our family relationships before Christ, we will at some point stumble in our pursuit of Him. Our relationships, possessions, culture, and satisfaction in life can and will become hindrances to our walk with Christ if we do not clearly and decisively put our relationship with Christ first. Dallas Willard, an American philosopher also known for his writings on Christian spiritual formation, reflected in his 1988 book *The Spirit of the Disciplines* on the absence of discipleship in the modern church says, "When Jesus walked among humankind, there was a certain simplicity to being a disciple. Primarily it meant to go with him in an attitude of study, obedience, and imitation ... The disciple is one who, intent upon becoming Christ-like and so dwelling in his 'faith and practice,' systematically and progressively rearranges his affairs to that end."[54]

2. Christian character is the bridge between the first and second commandments

In Matthew 22:37-40, Jesus says, "'Love the Lord your God with all your heart and with all your soul and with all your mind.' This is the first and greatest commandment. And the second is like it: 'Love your neighbor as yourself.' All the Law and the Prophets hang on these two commandments." When we love the Lord with all our heart, soul, and mind, we are transformed. The result is that we can then love our neighbor as ourselves. When we love the Lord, spend time with Him, and are transformed by the Holy Spirit, we become loving, not just superficially, but in the very depth of our being. The disciples were recognized because they acted just like their master. Jesus loved His disciples, they were enabled to love Him and love one another through His example, and then they were transformed by Jesus' love, empowered to love everyone with the same kind of love Jesus had for them.

Christian character is the natural result of loving the Lord. It is the evidence, the fruit, of love for God. Galatians 5:22-23 says "the fruit of the Spirit is love, joy, peace, forbearance, kindness, goodness, faithfulness, gentleness and self-control." These are the qualities produced within us as we walk with Christ. We don't *try* to become more loving; we simply *are* more loving. Transformation makes us able to love.

3. Character keeps us from legalism and rule keeping

Christ living within us produces freedom; freedom from bondage to sin, freedom to walk with Christ, and freedom from legalism. In Galatians 5, Paul contrasts life in the Spirit as being contrary to the sinful nature, saying that "if you are led by the Spirit, you are not under the law." (Galatians 5:18) He said this because the Galatians had descended into legalism, causing him to ask, "Did you receive the Spirit by the works of

---

54 Willard, pp. 260, 261.

the law, or by believing what you heard?" (Galatians 3:2) Legalism and rule keeping are the choices of our sinful nature.

4. The Christian church is meant to glorify Christ

When God's people are transformed, the Christian church becomes a place where Jesus is exalted and where peace reigns. When the Christian church is sinful, there are divisions and strife (Read 1 Corinthians 1:10-13). When we are led by the Spirit, we will get along with others. I'm not saying there will never be tension or times when we have to confront each other, but the atmosphere of the church will be one of growth and maturity. One of the sure signs in our lives that inner transformation is taking place is humility, the prerequisite for harmony in the Christian church.

I pastored churches for over twenty years. The greatest problem I saw in the church was interpersonal conflict. I dealt with people who didn't like each other and couldn't get along. In one church, I tried to bring two factions together, but my efforts fell short and the church never recovered. The only antidote for a church with strife is God's Holy Spirit.

5. Walking with God satisfies our soul

In the book *The Sacred Romance*, John Eldredge and Brent Curtis say that "on the outside, there is the external story of our lives. This is the life everyone sees, our life of work and play and church, of family and friends, paying bills, and growing older. There is a spiritual dimension to this external world in our desire to do good works, but communion with God is replaced by activity for God. There is little time in this outer world for deep questions. Given the right plan, everything in life can be managed...except your heart." They continue, "The inner life, the story of our heart, is the life of the deep places within us, our passions and dreams, our fears and our deepest wounds ... indeed, if we will listen, a Sacred Romance calls to us through our heart every moment of our lives. It whispers to us on the wind, invites us through the laughter of good friends, reaches out to us through the touch of someone we love. We've heard it in our favorite music, sensed it at the birth of our first child, been drawn to it while watching the shimmer of a sunset on the ocean. The Romance is even present in times of great personal suffering: the illness of a child, the loss of a marriage, the death of a friend. Something calls to us through experiences like these and rouses an inconsolable longing deep within our heart, wakening in us a yearning for intimacy, beauty, and adventure."[55]

The Lord created us with a God-shaped vacuum that can be filled only by His presence. Any other attempt will be temporary and partial. Adam and Eve had a perfectly satisfying existence in the Garden of Eden, but when they sinned, everything changed. God wants to be our all in all. Once we have just a glimpse of who God is, it becomes our life-long passion to find more of Him. American Christian pastor, preacher, and author A.W. Tozer wrote, "The man who has God for his treasure has all things in One. Many ordinary treasures may be denied him, or if he is allowed to have them, the enjoyment of them will be so tempered that they will never be necessary to his happiness. Or if he must see them go, one after one, he will scarcely feel a sense of loss, for having the Source of all things he has in One all satisfaction, all pleasure, all delight. Whatever he may lose he has actually lost nothing, for he now has it all in One, and he has it purely, legitimately and forever."[56] Walking with the Lord satisfies those deep places in our soul. God is restoring us to a place where we can experience again the Divine Romance.

6. We function correctly when we live in communion with Christ

God has given us clear directions in the Bible about how we ought to live, and when we live in the way which God has designed, the result is that we live a blessed life. In Deuteronomy 28, Moses gives the blessings for obedience to the Lord and the curses for disobedience to Him. For obedience, the nation of Israel would receive blessing for their children, their crops, and their livestock. They would have success against their enemies. They would become a special people in God's household. If, however, they disobeyed, they would be cursed in everything they did.

---

55 Curtis and Eldredge, *The Sacred Romance*, pp. 5-7.
56 Tozer, *The Pursuit of God*, kindle edition, location 170.

These admonitions apply to us today. When we don't live as God desires, we reap the consequences of our own disobedience. Christian character is simply living the way that God ordained for us to live.

Psalm 112:1-6 says, "Blessed are those who fear the Lord, who find great delight in his commands. Their children will be mighty in the land; the generation of the upright will be blessed. Wealth and riches are in their houses, and their righteousness endures forever. Even in darkness light dawns for the upright, for those who are gracious and compassionate and righteous. Good will come to those who are generous and lend freely, who conduct their affairs with justice. Surely the righteous will never be shaken; they will be remembered forever." It is clear that these blessings are a byproduct of searching after the Lord and putting Him first in our lives. As it says in Matthew 6:31-33, "Do not worry, saying, 'What shall we eat?' or 'What shall we drink?' or 'What shall we wear?' For the pagans run after all these things, and your heavenly Father knows that you need them. But seek first his kingdom and his righteousness, and all these things will be given to you as well." In communion with Christ, and only in communion with Christ, our lives are blessed and we function the way in which we were created to function.

7. A transformed life is attractive to non-believers

First Peter 2:12 exhorts Christians to "live such good lives among the pagans that, though they accuse you of doing wrong, they may see your good deeds and glorify God." Our lives are to be such good testimonies that when accusations are made against us, others will say the accusations don't fit what they know about our character. Christ in you is the most attractive thing in the whole world. Everyone knows deep inside that they are sinners, even if their theology and philosophy of life don't permit them to admit their own sinfulness. When they see us living a life which is dramatically and foundationally different from the best that they can come up with, they will be attracted to us.

Look no further than the life of Christ. Everywhere He went, people were drawn to Him. He was the most genuine, loving, intelligent, and patient person they had ever met. Jesus not only loved people unconditionally, He healed them, blessed them, and taught them truth. The crowds didn't come out of guilt or fear, but out of being drawn by Christ's love for them.

I had a friend whose oldest son was living in rebellion. I walked with this family through many years of disappointment as they watched their son indulge in drugs and alcohol, get involved in an affair, drift from one job to another, and live only for himself. The son had gone to a Christian school, grown up in a Christian family, and been loved and accepted through all his years of rebellion. Within the past few years, this same son started going to church and rededicated His life to Christ. He stopped drinking and doing drugs, joined the National Guard, and is responsible toward his family. The transformation is incredible and miraculous. His parents related to me how the example their son saw in other believers caused him to return to church, and ultimately, to the Lord.

8. Christian character avoids breakdown and chaos in our lives

I have seen many Christian leaders fall due to some type of character flaw—running off with money others gave to their ministry, getting involved in an affair, or being overwhelmed with power. Other Christians can't get along with co-workers, are rebellious toward authority, or allow a root of bitterness to take hold in their heart. Most of the problems in marriages, the workplace, the church, and in our social lives come from a breakdown of character.

I am part of a team working to help the Christian church in Turkey establish a solid character foundation in their congregations. We have initiated a project called the Timothy Project (Derin Değişim in Turkish, which means "deep change") in which Turks are writing indigenous discipleship materials for the Turkish church. We believe that in order to see the Turkish believers become mature they need to focus on character development early in their life of discipleship. Lessons have been written on issues like lying, honesty, righteousness, shame and honor (a big topic in a Muslim nation) and practical issues like husband-wife relations, child raising, sexuality, work ethics, and money. We are convinced that if a good character foundation is laid, knowledge and skills can be taught. If we are like Christ in our character, He will teach us what we need to know. A good foundation in character is the foundation to everything we do in life.

Making disciples

We cannot make disciples without being a disciple. This book has been devoted to studying what a disciple looks like when the process of discipleship is complete—when we are conformed to the image of Christ and become like Him. Like Paul, we are straining toward what is ahead, the prize for which God has called us heavenward in Christ Jesus (Philippians 3:14). I have not endeavored to talk about what the process of making disciples looks like, through a church discipleship or mentoring program. We can, however, glean a few principles to point the way to a better understanding of how to go about making disciples.

> We cannot make disciples without being a disciple.

If we are going to see inner transformation take place in someone else's life, we need to be in the process of transformation ourselves. We can only teach what we have learned. The first and most important tool we have is to live a life worth *imitating*. Those who are attracted to righteousness will be attracted to us when we exhibit a life which reflects Christ. In addition, we can *teach* others how to walk with Jesus, be led by Jesus, and learn from Jesus. If we can connect disciples with the power and presence of the Holy Spirit, He will teach, lead, instruct, and equip them. I would much rather disciple someone who has integrity of character, genuinely loves other people, and has a deep relationship with the Lord—but has not yet developed the skills for ministry or never been through formal theological education. In America we have concentrated on formal education and assumed that it provides adequate development of a person's character to begin ministry. I believe in formal education. I have many degrees and have benefitted greatly from formal academic training. However, character must come first.

Another vital component to making disciples is to develop within others a better understanding about the sinful nature. Too often, we do not focus on the dangers inherent in ministry, the reality of spiritual warfare, or the nature of this world's system. The five areas of Christ, Community, Character, Calling and Competencies (identified by Malcolm Webber on how to design a discipleship training program) and the four dynamics of spiritual, relational, experiential, and instructional discipleship are also vital. Webber's organization Leadersource offers different levels of training for those who want to construct a program for training leaders. These seminars are not intended to specify the specifics of the program you will design, but give the broad parameters which are needed to be designed so that inner transformation is the result. I strongly encourage you to contact Leadersource[57] to find training seminars in your area.

Finally, we need to be patient with those whom God has given us influence, instructing them one step at a time, restoring them and teaching them gently, and carrying their burdens and loving them to fullness in Christ. All of us have many areas in which we fall short in our Christian life; behavior, attitudes, values, worldview. It is easy to get discouraged with the depth of change needed. All of us have a long way to go. The most important thing we can give is unconditional love and an atmosphere of grace where they feel safe to make mistakes and be who they are, even while they are being changed.

Summary

Here are ten takeaways from this book for your life as a person of Christian character.

1. Transformation, not reformation of your ways or conformation to a different set of standards, is needed in your life. You need to be fundamentally changed in your nature, character, and worldview. You cannot add Christianity onto your existing beliefs and behaviors. We need a total remake of everything we are, beginning with a fundamental transformation in our inner being.

---

57 The website is: www.leadersouce.org

2. Character has to be Christian. You need to be born again in order to see inner transformation take place in your life. You need a new nature in order to lead a new life. You need the power of the Holy Spirit within you in order to see change. It takes the presence of Christ to reproduce the character of Christ in the inner being.

3. The foundation of all change is that God is good, is on your side, and desires the best for you. If we don't start with an embrace of God's goodness, we will tend toward legalism instead of transformation.

4. The most important character quality is love. You are to love the Lord with all your being, and love other people as yourself. Love is transformational.

5. God's Word and God's Holy Spirit reveal your sin and lead you into righteousness and spiritual freedom. Only as we encounter God's Word and His Spirit will we be spiritually transformed.

6. True freedom is the freedom *not* to sin. Sin destroys your life and keeps you in bondage to your sinful nature, in which there is nothing good. Only Christ can break the bondage of sin. Beholding Christ we will have the power to overcome Satan, the world, and our own sinful nature.

7. God is not trying to change your personality, but He is changing your character for His glory.

8. A transformed life is the only life that will satisfy you at the deepest level of who you are. Only in a Sacred Romance with God Himself will you have purpose, satisfaction, and victory in your life. Christ died not just so that you will go to heaven when you die (although you will if you have received Christ into your life) but so that you will be fulfilled while on this earth, you will be fruitful in other people's lives, and so that you will be useful as an instrument to usher in the Kingdom of Heaven to this earth.

9. Suffering is one of the tools God uses to infuse His power into your weakness. God is more concerned with your character than with your comfort.

10. The only answer for sin is Christ, who paid the penalty for your sin, provided justification for your sin, was your substitute for sin, took

the punishment for your sin on Himself, gave you a new nature and sent the Holy Spirit to be your teacher and guide you into truth.

Inner transformation or sanctification is the tool which God uses in order to get us to the place of freedom, joy, love, and fruitfulness. We have looked at the process of inner transformation from all kinds of different angles. You are precious in the eyes of the Lord, and He wants to give you not just eternal life, not just a heavenly home, but a victorious, blessed, fulfilling, fruitful life in this present age. He has more for you than you can ever imagine. God wants to turn you into a butterfly, free to become all that He intended you to be. Everything He wants for you is good for you and will lead to freedom, joy, and productiveness in your life.

In this volume, I have set out to demonstrate what biblical character is about and to define Christian character as the end goal of your Christian life. You were designed by God to live only in communion with Him. True character comes from God and is only worked into your life through an ongoing, born-again relationship with Him. When my wife Caroline and I were born again all those years ago in the hippie commune, we would never have anticipated the incredible journey God has given us in the five decades since that life-changing day. In our quest to seek truth from the One who calls Himself the truth, we have been remade in the image of God, and have done our utmost to live with Christian character.

This volume has looked in depth at the issue of inner transformation and sets the stage for Volume Two where we will discuss the specifics of what Christian character is all about. What are we supposed to look like when God transforms us into butterflies? We will examine in depth negative character qualities (e.g. the sinful nature) as well as positive character qualities (e.g. the fruit of the Spirit). We will look at behaviors as well as values, character qualities, and attitudes which exemplify the Christian life.

Now we ask you to finish the quest. If you are a born again Christian and this book has challenged you to make some significant changes in your life and your relationship with God, I urge you to obey the Lord's leading and allow Him to transform you anew from the inside out. If you are a churchgoer, or even someone who has never stepped foot into a church, and feel within you a stirring to know the true God who give you true character—please ask Jesus Christ to come into your life as your Lord and Savior. It'll be the greatest and most fulfilling decision you've ever made.

As we contemplate the topic of Christian character, let's remember the One who is perfect, who gave His life so that we could be remade into the image of God—Jesus Christ. He not only showed us in His person who God is, what His character is like, and demonstrated how we ought to live our lives to bring glory to God; He also gave us the ability, through His Spirit and through new birth, to become like God.

Colossians 3:18 says, "And we, who with unveiled faces all reflect the Lord's glory, are being transformed into his likeness with ever-increasing glory, which comes from the Lord, who is the Spirit." Since God is absolutely perfect in character, our joy as Christians is that as we are transformed into his likeness we are also set free to become what we have never even dreamed we could be - butterflies set free to bring glory to God. Ephesians 3:20,21 says, "Now to him who is able to do immeasurably more than all we ask or imagine, according to his power that is at work within us, to him be glory in the church and in Christ Jesus throughout all generations, for ever and ever! Amen."

ABOUT THE AUTHOR

Frank Martin has a passion for preaching and teaching the Word of God. He received his bachelor's degree from Miami University in Oxford, Ohio, his master's of divinity degree from Gordon-Conwell Theological Seminary, and his doctor of ministry degree from Phoenix Seminary. Frank was a pastor for twenty-two years: five years on the east coast, fifteen years at Saguaro Canyon Evangelical Free Church in Tucson, AZ, and two years as an interim pastor in Benson, AZ. Since 2004, Frank has been working full-time as a missionary with the International Turkey Network and on the Timothy Project developing indigenous discipleship materials for the church in Turkey. He also is working with the Orality Project, promoting oral methodology in Turkey. He and his wife Caroline (an elementary and secondary school teacher and principal) have targeted church planting work in the northern Aegean region of Turkey. More recently they have been working with refugees both in Turkey and in Tucson, Arizona. They have two children, Amy and Matthew (who is married to Kirsten), and his entire family lives in Tucson, Arizona.

APPENDIX

TRAITS OF UNGODLY THINKING

TRAIT	PASSAGES
Futile	Romans 1:21 For although they knew God, they neither glorified him as God nor gave thanks to him, but their thinking became futile and their foolish hearts were darkened. 1 Corinthians 3:20 and again, "The Lord knows that the thoughts of the wise are futile." Ephesians 4:17 So I tell you this, and insist on it in the Lord, that you must no longer live as the Gentiles do, in the futility of their thinking.
Darkened	Romans 1:21 For although they knew God, they neither glorified him as God nor gave thanks to him, but their thinking became futile and their foolish hearts were darkened. Ephesians 4:18 They are darkened in their understanding and separated from the life of God because of the ignorance that is in them due to the hardening of their hearts.
Separated from the life of God	Ephesians 4:18 They are darkened in their understanding and separated from the life of God because of the ignorance that is in them due to the hardening of their hearts.
Hardened hearts	Romans 1:21 For although they knew God, they neither glorified him as God nor gave thanks to him, but their thinking became futile and their foolish hearts were darkened. Ephesians 4:18 They are darkened in their understanding and separated from the life of God because of the ignorance that is in them due to the hardening of their hearts.
Ignorant	Ephesians 4:18 They are darkened in their understanding and separated from the life of God because of the ignorance that is in them due to the hardening of their hearts.
Foolish	Romans 1:22 Although they claimed to be wise, they became fools
Believe lies	Romans 1: 25 They exchanged the truth of God for a lie, and worshiped and served created things rather than the Creator— who is forever praised. Amen. John 8:44 You belong to your father, the devil, and you want to carry out your father's desire. He was a murderer from the beginning, not holding to the truth, for there is no truth in him. When he lies, he speaks his native language, for he is a liar and the father of lies.

TRAIT	PASSAGES
Depraved	Romans 1:28 Furthermore, since they did not think it worthwhile to retain the knowledge of God, he gave them over to a depraved mind, to do what ought not to be done. 2 Timothy 3:8 Just as Jannes and Jambres opposed Moses, so also these men oppose the truth— men of depraved minds, who, as far as the faith is concerned, are rejected.
Minds set on what the sinful nature desires	Romans 8:5 Those who live according to the sinful nature have their minds set on what that nature desires; but those who live in accordance with the Spirit have their minds set on what the Spirit desires.
Dull	2 Corinthians 3:14 But their minds were made dull, for to this day the same veil remains when the old covenant is read. It has not been removed, because only in Christ is it taken away.
Led astray	2 Corinthians 11:3 But I am afraid that just as Eve was deceived by the serpent's cunning, your minds may somehow be led astray from your sincere and pure devotion to Christ.
Enemies of God	Colossians 1:21 Once you were alienated from God and were enemies in your minds because of your evil behavior.
Set on earthly things	Colossians 3:2 Set your minds on things above, not on earthly things.
Impure	Titus 1:15 To the pure, all things are pure, but to those who are corrupted and do not believe, nothing is pure. In fact, both their minds and consciences are corrupted.
Corrupted	Titus 1:15 To the pure, all things are pure, but to those who are corrupted and do not believe, nothing is pure. In fact, both their minds and consciences are corrupted.
Conforms to the pattern of this world	Romans 12:2 Do not conform any longer to the pattern of this world, but be transformed by the renewing of your mind. Then you will be able to test and approve what God's will is— his good, pleasing and perfect will.
Leads to death	Romans 8:6 The mind of sinful man is death, but the mind controlled by the Spirit is life and peace;
Set on what the sinful nature desires	Romans 8:5 Those who live according to the sinful nature have their minds set on what that nature desires; but those who live in accordance with the Spirit have their minds set on what the Spirit desires.
Hostile to God	Romans 8:7 The sinful mind is hostile to God. It does not submit to God's law, nor can it do so.

TRAIT	PASSAGES
Doesn't submit to God's law	Romans 8:7 The sinful mind is hostile to God. It does not submit to God's law, nor can it do so
Cannot submit to God's law	Romans 8:7 the sinful mind is hostile to God. It does not submit to God's law, nor can it do so.

TRAITS OF GODLY THINKING

TRAIT	PASSAGES
Glorify God	Romans 1:21 For although they knew God, they neither glorified him as God nor gave thanks to him, but their thinking became futile and their foolish hearts were darkened.
Give thanks to God	Romans 1:21 For although they knew God, they neither glorified him as God nor gave thanks to him, but their thinking became futile and their foolish hearts were darkened.
Wise	Matthew 7:24 "Therefore everyone who hears these words of mine and puts them into practice is like a wise man who built his house on the rock. 2 Timothy 3:14,15 But as for you, continue in what you have learned and have become convinced of, because you know those from whom you learned it, and how from infancy you have known the holy Scriptures, which are able to make you wise for salvation through faith in Christ Jesus.
Produce good fruit	James 3:17 But the wisdom that comes from heaven is first of all pure; then peace-loving, considerate, submissive, full of mercy and good fruit, impartial and sincere.
Pure	James 3:17 But the wisdom that comes from heaven is first of all pure; then peace-loving, considerate, submissive, full of mercy and good fruit, impartial and sincere.
Peace-loving	James 3:17 But the wisdom that comes from heaven is first of all pure; then peace-loving, considerate, submissive, full of mercy and good fruit, impartial and sincere.
Considerate	James 3:17 But the wisdom that comes from heaven is first of all pure; then peace-loving, considerate, submissive, full of mercy and good fruit, impartial and sincere.
Submissive	James 3:17 But the wisdom that comes from heaven is first of all pure; then peace-loving, considerate, submissive, full of mercy and good fruit, impartial and sincere.

TRAIT	PASSAGES
Full of mercy	James 3:17 But the wisdom that comes from heaven is first of all pure; then peace-loving, considerate, submissive, full of mercy and good fruit, impartial and sincere.
Impartial	James 3:17 But the wisdom that comes from heaven is first of all pure; then peace-loving, considerate, submissive, full of mercy and good fruit, impartial and sincere.
Sincere	James 3:17 But the wisdom that comes from heaven is first of all pure; then peace-loving, considerate, submissive, full of mercy and good fruit, impartial and sincere.
Adult like	1 Corinthians 14:20 Brothers, stop thinking like children. In regard to evil be infants, but in your thinking be adults.
Wholesome	2 Peter 3:1 Dear friends, this is now my second letter to you. I have written both of them as reminders to stimulate you to wholesome thinking.
Enlightened	Ephesians 1:18 I pray also that the eyes of your heart may be enlightened in order that you may know the hope to which he has called you, the riches of his glorious inheritance in the saints,
Set on what the Spirit desires	Romans 8:5 Those who live according to the sinful nature have their minds set on what that nature desires; but those who live in accordance with the Spirit have their minds set on what the Spirit desires.
Life and peace	Romans 8:6 The mind of sinful man is death, but the mind controlled by the Spirit is life and peace;
In accord with the Truth	John 8:31,32 To the Jews who had believed him, Jesus said, "If you hold to my teaching, you are really my disciples. Then you will know the truth, and the truth will set you free." John 14:16,17 And I will ask the Father, and he will give you another Counselor to be with you forever—the Spirit of truth. The world cannot accept him, because it neither sees him nor knows him. But you know him, for he lives with you and will be in you. John 16:13 But when he, the Spirit of truth, comes, he will guide you into all truth. He will not speak on his own; he will speak only what he hears, and he will tell you what is yet to come. John 17:17 Sanctify them by the truth; your word is truth. Romans 1:25 They exchanged the truth of God for a lie, and worshiped and served created things rather than the Creator— who is forever praised. Amen.

WORKS CITED

(VOLUMES ONE AND TWO)

Anderson, Francis I., and Donald G. Wiseman. *Tyndale Old Testament Commentaries: Job: An Introduction and Commentary*. London, Downer's Grove, ILL: Intervarsity, 1976. Print.

Arndt, William, F. Wilbur Gingrich, Frederick W. Danker, and Walter Bauer. *A Greek-English Lexicon of the New Testament and Other Early Christian Literature: A Translation and Adaptation of the Fourth Revised and Augmented Edition of Walter Bauer's Griechisch-deutsches Wörterbuch Zu Den Schriften Des Neuen Testaments Und Der übrigen Urchristlichen Literatur*. Chicago: U of Chicago, 1979. Print.

Baer, Randall N. *Inside the New Age Nightmare*. Lafayette, LA: Huntington House, 1989. Print.

Barclay, William. *Flesh and Spirit*. Nashville: Abingdon, 1962. Print.

Barna, George. *Maximum Faith: Live like Jesus, Experience Genuine Transformation*. Brentwood, TN: Published in Association with the Literary Agency of Fedd, 2011. Print.

Barrett, C.K. *The First Epistle to the Corinthians*. New York, Hagerstown, San Francisco, London: Harper & Row, 1968. Print.

Barrett, C.K. *The First Epistle to the Corinthians*. New York, Hagerstown, San Francisco, London: Harper & Row, 1968. Print.

Berkhof, Louis. *Systematic Theology*. Boston: William B. Eerdmans, 1976. Print.

Bible Works for Windows. Vers. 4.0.035p. N.p.: BibleWorks, LCC, 1998. Computer software.

Blamires, Harry. *The Christian Mind: How Should a Christian Think?* Ann Arbor, MI: Servant, 1963. Print.

Bonhoeffer, Dietrich, and Eberhard Bethge. *Letters and Papers from Prison*. New York: Macmillan, 1972. Print.

Bonhoeffer, Dietrich. *The Cost of Discipleship*. New York: Touchstone, 1995. Print.

Brooks, Thomas. *The Classic Works of Thomas Brooks*. Kindle Edition ed. N.p.: Kindle, 1680. Print.

Brown, Colin. *The New International Dictionary of New Testament Theology*. Vol. 1-3. Grand Rapids, MI: Zondervan Pub. House, 1975. Print.

Brown, Raymond Edward. *The Gospel According to John*. Vol. 1 & 2. Garden City, NY: Doubleday, 1966. Print.

Bruce, F. F. *The Epistles to the Colossians, Philemon and to the Ephesians*. Grand Rapids: William B. Eerdmans, 1984. Print. The New International Commentary on the New Testament.

Bruce, F.F. *Commentary on Galatians*. Grand Rapids, MI: Eerdmans, 1982. Print.

Burns, James, and Andrew Watterson Blackwood. *Revivals: Their Laws and Leaders*. Grand Rapids: Baker Book House, 1960. Print.

Calvijn, Johannes, John Thomas MacNeill, and Ford Lewis Battles. *Institutes of the Christian Religion: In Two Volumes*. Philadelphia: Westminster, 1960. Print.

Carson, D. A. *The Intolerance of Tolerance*. Grand Rapids, MI: William B. Eerdmans Pub., 2012. Print.

Chambers, Oswald. *My Utmost for His Highest*. E-book ed. Grand Rapids, MI: Discovery House, 1963. Print. November, 2010.

Chambers, Oswald. *Studies in the Sermon on the Mount: God's Character and the Believer's Conduct*. Grand Rapids, MI: Discovery House, 1995. Print.

Chambers, Oswald. *Studies in the Sermon on the Mount. (This Edition 1960 ... Third Impression.)*. London: Oswald Chambers Publications Association; Marshall, Morgan & Scott, 1972. Print.

Clowney, Edmund P. *The Message of 1 Peter : The Way of the Cross*. Ed. John R. Stott. New York: InterVarsity, 1989. Print.

Colson, Charles W., and Ellen Santilli. Vaughn. *Against the Night: Living in the New Dark Ages*. Ann Arbor, MI: Vine, 1989. Print.

Colson, Charles W. *Loving God*. Grand Rapids, MI: Zondervan Pub. House, 1983. Print.

Crabb, Lawrence J. *Inside out*. Colorado Springs, CO: NavPress, 1988. Print.

Craigie, Peter C. *The Book of Deuteronomy*. Grand Rapids: Wm. B. Eerdmans, 1976. Print. The New Testament Commentary on the Old Testament.

Craigie, Peter C. *Psalms 1-50*. Grand Rapids: Paternoster, 1986. Print.

Cranfield, C.E.B. *The Epistle to the Romans*. Vol. 1 & 2. Edinburgh: T & T Clark Limited, 1981. Print.

Curtis, Brent, and John Eldredge. *The Sacred Romance: Drawing Closer to the Heart of God*. Nashville: Thomas Nelson, 1997. Print.

Darwin, Charles. *Origin of the Species*. N.p.: n.p., 1857. Kindle Edition.

Dieter, Melvin Easterday. *Five Views on Sanctification*. Grand Rapids, MI: Academie, 1987. Print.

Dillow, Joseph C. *The Reign of the Servant Kings: A Study of Eternal Security and the Final Significance of Man*. 2nd ed. Hayesville, NC: Schoettle Pub., 1993. Print.

Douglas, J. D. *The New International Dictionary of the Christian Church*. Grand Rapids: Zondervan Pub., 1978. Print.

Durham, John I. *Exodus*. Grand Rapids: Paternoster, 1986. Print.

Fee, Gordon D. *The First Epistle to the Corinthians*. Grand Rapids, MI: W.B. Eerdmans Pub., 1987. Print.

Foster, Richard J., and James Bryan. Smith. *Devotional Classics: Selected Readings for Individuals and Groups*. [San Francisco]: HarperSanFrancisco, 2005. Print.

Foster, Richard J. *Celebration of Discipline: The Path to Spiritual Growth*. San Francisco: Harper & Row, 1988. Print.

Fung, Ronald Y.K. *The Epistle to the Galatians*. Grand Rapids, MI: W.B. Eerdmans Pub., 1988. Print.

Gleason, Randall. "B. B. Warfield and Lewis S. Chafer on Sanctification." *Journal of the Evangelical Theological Society* 40.2 (1997): 241-56. *ATLAS Serials*. Web. 7 May 2013. <http://ATLA.com>.

Golding, William. *Lord of the Flies*. New York: Coward-McCann, 1962. Print.

Grimm, Carl Ludwig Wilibald, Joseph Henry Thayer, and Christian Gottlob Wilke. *Greek-English Lexicon of the New Testament: Being Grimm's Wilke's Clavis Novi Testamenti*. Grand Rapids, MI: Zondervan, 1979. Print.

Groothuis, Douglas R. *Unmasking the New Age*. Downers Grove, IL: InterVarsity, 1986. Print.

Grudem, Wayne A. *The First Epistle of Peter: An Introduction and Commentary*. Leicester, England: Inter-Varsity, 1988. Print.

Grudem, Wayne A. *The First Epistle of Peter: An Introduction and Commentary*. Leicester, England: Inter-Varsity, 1988. Print.

Grudem, Wayne A. *Systematic Theology: An Introduction to Biblical Doctrine*. Grand Rapids, MI: Zondervan, 2000. Print.

Guinness, Os, Virginia Mooney, and Karen Lee-Thorp. *When No One Sees: The Importance of Character in an Age of Image*. Colorado Springs, CO: Navpress, 2000. Print.

Guthrie, Donald. *New Testament Theology*. Leicester, England: Inter-Varsity, 1981. Print.

Harris, R. Laird, Gleason L. Archer, and Bruce K. Waltke. *Theological Wordbook of the Old Testament*. Vol. 1, 2. Chicago: Moody, 1980. Print.

Hixson, J. B., Rick Whitmire, and Roy B. Zuck. *Freely by His Grace: Classical Free Grace Theology*. Duluth, MN: Grace Gospel, 2012. Print.

Houston, J. M. *I Believe in the Creator*. Grand Rapids: Eerdmans, 1980. Print.

Hunter, James Davison. *The Death of Character: Moral Education in an Age without Good or Evil*. New York: Basic, 2000. Print.

Keller, Timothy J. *The Prodigal God: Recovering the Heart of the Christian Faith.* New York: Dutton, 2008. Print.

Kempis, Thomas A. *The Imitation of Christ.* N.p.: n.p., 1400. Kindle Edition.

Kurtz, Paul. *The Fullness of Life.* New York: Horizon, 1974. Print.

Lamont, Corliss. *The Philosophy of Humanism.* New York: Continuum, 1990. Print.

Lewis, C. S. *The Complete C.S. Lewis Signature Classics.* [San Francisco, Calif.]: HarperSanFrancisco, 2002. Print.

Lewis, Clive Staples. *Mere Christianity: A Revised and Enlarged Edition, with a New Introduction, of the Three Books The Case for Christianity, Christian Behaviour, and Beyond Personality.* New York: Macmillan, 1960. Print.

Lloyd-Jones, David Martyn. *Studies in the Sermon on the Mount.* Grand Rapids, MI: Eerdmans, 1976. Print.

Longenecker, Richard N. *Galatians.* Dallas, TX: Word, 1990. Print.

Manning, Brennan. *Ruthless Trust: The Ragamuffin's Path to God.* San Francisco: HarperCollins, 2002. Print.

Marshall, I. Howard. *1 and 2 Thessalonians: Based on the Revised Standard Version.* Grand Rapids [Mich.: Eerdmans, 1983. Print.

McKechnie, Jean Lyttleton, and Noah Webster. *Webster's New Universal Unabridged Dictionary: Based upon the Broad Foundations Laid down by Noah Webster.* 2nd ed. Cleveland, OH: Dorset & Baber, 1983. Print.

Michaels, J. Ramsey. *1 Peter.* Grand Rapids: Paternoster, 1988. Print.

Morris, Leon. *The Gospel According to John; the English Text with Introduction, Exposition and Notes.* Grand Rapids: Eerdmans, 1971. Print.

Morris, Leon. *The Gospel According to Matthew.* Grand Rapids, MI: William B. Eerdmans, 1992. Print.

Mostrom, Donald G. *Spiritual Privileges You Didn't Know Were Yours.* Downers Grove, IL: InterVarsity, 1986. Print.

Motyer, J. A. *The Message of Philippians.* Downers Grove, IL: Inter-Varsity, 1984. Print.

Musk, Bill Andrew. *The Unseen Face of Islam: Sharing the Gospel with Ordinary Muslims.* Eastbourne, E. Sussex: MARC, Evangelical Missionary Alliance, 1989. Print.

The NIV Study Bible. Grand Rapids: Zondervan Corporation, 1995. Print.

Noebel, David A. *Understanding the Times: The Religious Worldviews of Our Day and the Search for Truth.* Manitou Springs, CO: Summit, 1991. Print.

Packer, J. I. *Knowing God.* Downers Grove, IL: InterVarsity, 1973. Print.

Packer, J. I. *Knowing God.* Downers Grove, IL: InterVarsity, 1973. Print.

Pink, Arthur Walkington. *The Attributes of God*. Kindle ed. Grand Rapids: Baker, 1975. Print.

Pitts, Edward L. "Holding the Line." Editorial. *World Magazine* 13 July 2013: 34-38. Print.

Prager, Dennis. "Still the Best Hope: Why the World Needs American Values to Triumph." *Goodreads*. Broadside Books, May 2012. Web. 06 Aug. 2012. <http://www.goodreads.com/book/show/13379396-still-the-best-hope>.

Prager, Dennis. "Who Is Happy?" *Creators Syndicate* March 13 (2012): n. pag. Web. 25 Mar. 2012. <http://www.creators.com>.

Random House Webster's College Dictionary. New York: Random House, 1997. Print.

Samenow, Stanton E. *Inside the Criminal Mind*. New York: Times, 1984. Print.

Sanders, J. Oswald. *Spiritual Leadership*. Chicago: Moody, 1994. Print.

Sanders, J. Oswald. *Spiritual Maturity*. Chicago: Moody, 1969. Print.

Scazzero, Peter. *Emotionally Healthy Spirituality: Unleash a Revolution in Your Life in Christ*. Nashville, TN: Integrity, 2006. Print.

Schmidt, Alvin J. *How Christianity Changed the World: Formerly Titled Under the Influence*. Grand Rapids, MI: Zondervan, 2004. Print.

Smedes, Lewis B. *Love Within Limits : A Realist's View of I Corinthians 13*. Boston: William B. Eerdmans, 1978. Print.

Smith, F. LaGard. *The Narrated Bible in Chronological Order*. Eugene: Harvest House, 1984. Print.

Solzhenitsyn, Aleksandr Isaevich. *The Gulag Archipelago, 1918-1956: An Experiment in Literary Investigation*. New York: Harper & Row, 1974. Print.

Sproul, R. C., and Abdul Saleeb. *The Dark Side of Islam*. Wheaton: Crossway Bibles, 2005. Print.

Spurgeon, C. H. *The Treasury of David: Containing an Original Exposition of the Book of Psalms : A Collection of Illustrative Extracts from the Whole Range of Literature : A Series of Homiletical Hints upon Almost Every Verse ; and Lists of Writers upon Each Psalm*. McLean, VA: Macdonald Pub., [19-. Print.

Spurgeon, C. H. *The Treasury of David: Containing an Original Exposition of the Book of Psalms: A Collection of Illustrative Extracts from the Whole Range of Literature: A Series of Homiletical Hints upon Almost Every Verse ; and Lists of Writers upon Each Psalm*. McLean, VA: Macdonald Pub., n.d. Print.

Stott, John R. *The Message of Ephesians*. Ed. J. Alec Motyer. New York: InterVarsity, 1984. Print.

Stott, John R. W., and John R. W. Stott. *The Message of the Sermon on the Mount (Matthew 5-7): Christian Counter-culture*. Leicester [Leicestershire: Inter-varsity, 1985. Print.

Stuter, Lynn M. "Third Force Psychology in the Classroom." *Third Force Psychology in the Classroom*. N.p., Apr. 1996. Web. 14 May 2012. <http://www.learn-usa.com/education_transformation/er005.htm>.

Swindoll, Charles R. *Tale of the Tardy Oxcart and 1501 Other Stories: A Collection of Stories, Anecdotes, Illustrations, and Quotes*. Nashville, TN: Word Pub., 1998. Print.

Thomas, Cal. *The Death of Ethics in America*. Waco: Word, 1988. Print.

Thrall, Bill, Bruce McNicol, and Ken McElrath. *The Ascent of a Leader: How Ordinary Relationships Develop Extraordinary Character and Influence*. San Francisco, CA: Jossey-Bass, 1999. Print.

Tournier, Paul. *The Meaning of Persons*. San Francisco: Harper & Row, 1957. Print.

Tournier, Paul. *Reflections: On Life's Most Crucial Questions*. New York: Harper & Row, 1976. Print.

Tozer, A. W. *The Pursuit of God;*. Harrisburg, PA: Christian Publications, 1948. Kindle.

Tozer, A.W. *Attriues of God*. Kindle ed. Vol. 1. N.p.: n.p., n.d. Print.

Trevethan, Thomas L. *Our Joyful Confidence: The Lordship of Jesus in Colossians*. Downers Grove: InterVarsity, 1981. Print.

Vine, W. E. *An Expository Dictionary of New Testament Words with Their Precise Meanings for English Readers,*. Old Tappan, NJ: Revell, 1966. Print.

Warren, Rick. *The Purpose Driven Life : What on Earth Am I Here For?* Grand Rapids: Zondervan, 2002. Print.

Wenham, Gordon J. *The Book of Leviticus*. Grand Rapids, MI: W.B. Eerdmans, 1979. Print.

Wesley, John. *A Plain Account of Christian Perfection*. London: Kindle Books, 27 Jan. 1767.

Wiley, H. Orton. *Christian Theology*. Vol. 1 - 3. Kansas City: Beacon Hill, 1940. Print.

Willard, Dallas. *The Spirit of the Disciplines: Understanding How God Changes Lives*. San Francisco: HarperSanFrancisco, 1991. Print.

Wuest, Kenneth. *Bypaths in the Greek New Testament*. Grand Rapids, Michigan: Wm. B. Eerdmans, 1978. Print.

Wuest, Kenneth S. *Word Studies in the Greek New Testament*. Boston: William B. Eerdmans, 1973. Print.

Yancey, Philip. *The Jesus I Never Knew*. Grand Rapids, MI: Zondervan Pub. House, 1995. Print.

pg 55 line 10 foolish ! it

Made in the USA
San Bernardino, CA
26 August 2017